IMAGES
of America

AMADOR COUNTY

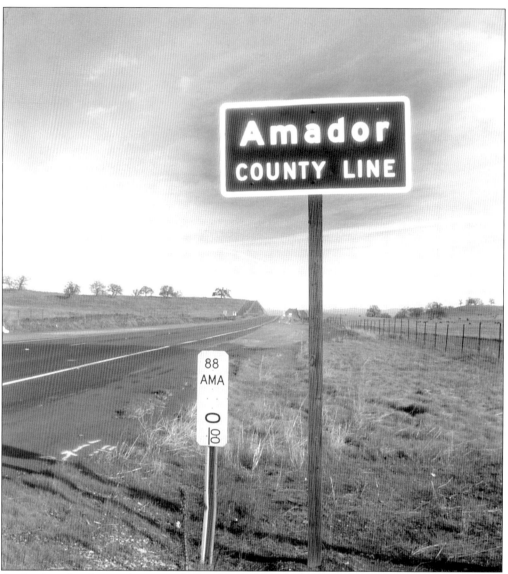

At the Amador County line, seen here coming in from San Joaquin County, one enters a place where gold country history still lives amid beautiful forested hills, rivers, quaint hamlets, and modern towns.

ON THE COVER: Participants in the Horrible Parade, on a float driven by Lideo Valvo, gear up for their appearance on July 4, 1929, at the present-day location of Piccardo Way in Jackson. (See page 13 for more of this image.)

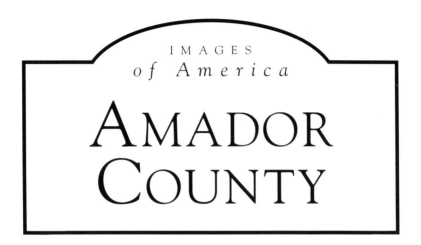

IMAGES
of America

AMADOR
COUNTY

John Poultney and
the Amador County Archives

ARCADIA
PUBLISHING

Published by Arcadia Publishing
Charleston SC, Chicago IL, Portsmouth NH, San Francisco CA

Printed in the United States of America

Library of Congress Catalog Card Number: 2006933245

For all general information contact Arcadia Publishing at:
Telephone 843-853-2070
Fax 843-853-0044
E-mail sales@arcadiapublishing.com
For customer service and orders:
Toll-Free 1-888-313-2665

Visit us on the Internet at www.arcadiapublishing.com

For Tom and Nate. May you be intrepid, and enjoy Amador and the great outdoors. If you ever get overwhelmed, just remember Jane Austen's words, "To sit in the shade on a fine day and look upon verdure is the most perfect refreshment."

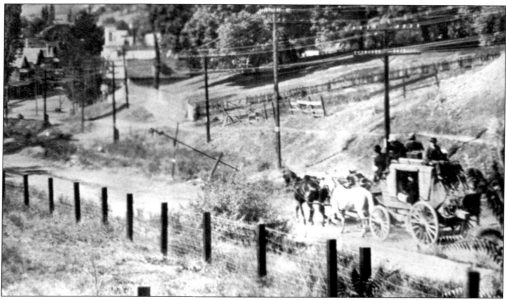

In the 1800s, horse-driven stage was the best way to get around the foothills. Despite the rough terrain, they provided smooth passage due to surprisingly sophisticated shock-absorbing systems. Here a stage laden with well-dressed travelers approaches the outskirts of Sutter Creek c. 1900. (Courtesy Amador County Archives.)

CONTENTS

ACKNOWLEDGMENTS

I am deeply indebted to Larry Cenotto and Deborah C. Cook at the Amador County Archives for their knowledge of things Amador and for letting me hog six feet of counter space with my scanner for hours at a time. I also wish to thank Terry Grillo for his photographs and knowledge of history, expert photographer Bill Lavallie for his fine contemporary images, Greg Bortolin and Bonnie Kuczborski for cool knickknacks and for turning me on to Amador in the first place, the Jackson Rancheria, Tommy Maguire for the photograph of Brian Setzer, Kimberly Wooten for her Amador knowledge (check out her book *Sutter Creek*), my wife, Lori, for her encouragement and patience through this project, my sons Tom and Nate for putting up with me ignoring them while writing captions late at night, Matthew and Lori Hedger of Volcano for the Volcano etching, Brian Swanson of PG&E in San Francisco for the Tiger Creek and Mokelumne River Project photographs, Donna Raskin for inspiring me, Stefano Watson at Avio Vineyards for wine and history, and the Amador County Department of Surveying and Mapping for the cool 1866 map.

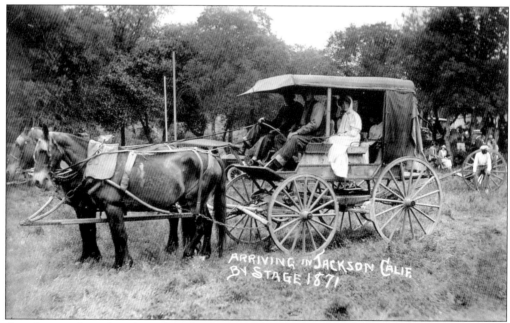

Amador travelers often dressed to the nines for rides along the dusty roads. (Courtesy Amador County Archives.)

INTRODUCTION

A person would consider oneself lucky just to know about Amador County and luckier still having the pleasure to visit. This smallish county of woodlands, foothills, mountains, farms, and cities, bracketed by the Cosumnes and Mokelumne Rivers, has some of California's best scenery and more than a little bit of history. Amador is the only county in the state named for a non-Indian native Californian, Jose Maria Amador, a wealthy ranchero who had a large ranch in the Bay Area near what are now Danville and Livermore. The area of his ranch in that part of the state, in Contra Costa County, is now named Amador Valley. During the gold rush, some of his employees were prospecting in a creek and named it Amadore's Creek. Soon thereafter, the camps of Amadore Crossing and South Amadore (now Amador City) sprang up, and the miners proposed in 1852 that the new county be called "Amador." This name won out over "Washington" when the county was finally incorporated in 1854.

Today's Amador can be considered a modern suburban area, and it bears little resemblance to the halcyon gold-mining days. That's why a book like this is of interest. In these pages a person will see an Amador that doesn't really exist anymore, despite some excellent preservation efforts that maintain some of the area's original structures. Life has changed, and the pace of towns like Jackson, Sutter Creek, Pioneer, and Pine Grove isn't so slow anymore. Housing developments, big box retailers, and industrial parks are moving in, and eternal vigilance is needed to help keep Amador's original flavor. This book tries to capture that essence by showing people going about their everyday lives in the old days, with a smattering of modern images for comparison.

Here's the twist: despite appearances, this isn't really a history book. To encapsulate the entire history of this complicated place in one volume is disingenuous at best, and several people told me I was crazy to even try. They said complete books could, and should, be done just on the county's mining history, or just on the Amador Central Railroad, or just on Jackson, or just on Pine Grove. And they're right. One might critique this collection of images as somewhat random, but such is the nature of life. This book is meant to show regular people rather than focusing on the giants of industry or civic leaders. Those books have already been done and done well. So if the search is for a truly focused, linear history of Amador, take a look at Larry Cenotto's impressive multivolume *Logan's Alley*, or drill down into the towns with Kimberly Wooten and R. Scott Baxter's *Sutter Creek* or Elaine Zorbas's *Fiddletown: From Gold Rush to Rediscovery*. For a truly harrowing and fascinating read, check out *47 Down: The 1922 Argonaut Gold Mine Disaster* by O. Henry Mace. Any of these books gets into much greater detail than is possible with a survey of captions and photographs. And keep those eyes peeled for more Amador books—this is a fascinating place with a lot more to discover. Send comments and critiques to john_poultney@yahoo.com.

Onward!

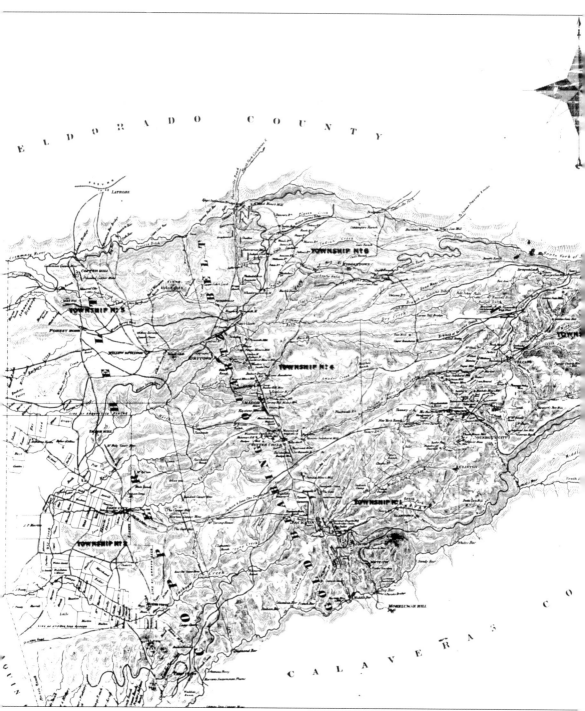

Amador County was formed on June 11, 1854, as an act of the California legislature, then located in San Jose. The county was formed by dividing Calaveras County, with the northern border being Dry Creek near today's Drytown. A small portion of Alpine County was originally part of Amador but was ceded by legislation to Alpine in 1864. This is the official county map from 1866, the borders of which still apply. The "townships" here correspond to the modern-day towns

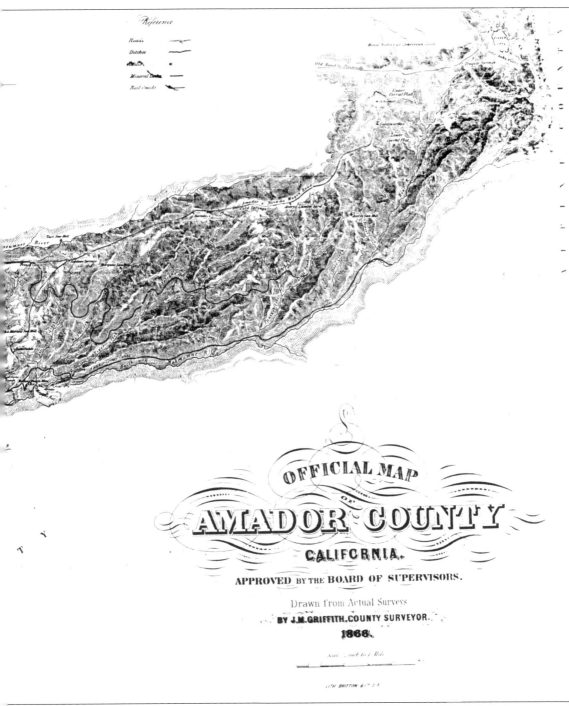

like Jackson, Pine Grove, Volcano, and Sutter Creek but originally indicated political subdivision containing two or more cities, each with two justices and two constables. Note that the hilly area north from Mokelumne Hill to Drytown reads "Gold Bearing Quartz Belt" and that the hills to the west of Jackson read "Copper Belt." (Courtesy Amador County Department of Surveying and Mapping.)

9

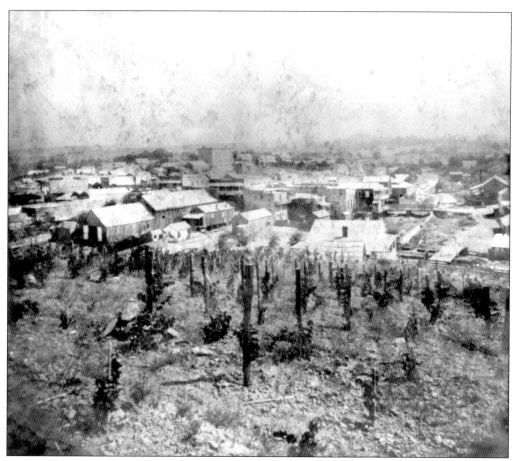

Jackson, pictured here in 1866, was founded in 1848 at a spring at the current site of the National Hotel and named for Col. Alden Jackson. The town quickly became a gold-country mecca, as it was in one of the richest gold-producing areas of the Sierra Nevada. This image is the first known of the city after an 1862 fire almost completely destroyed Jackson. The courthouse is the large building near left center, and the National Hotel is the darkened building near right center, just above the rooftop with the prominent chimney. The grapes in the foreground foreshadow Amador's development into a prominent wine region. (Courtesy Amador County Archives.)

One

MAIN DRAGS,
BACK ALLEYS,
AND FRONT PORCHES

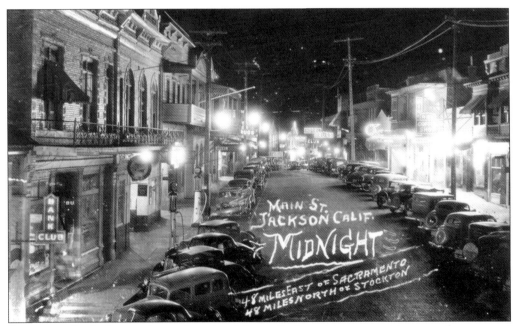

Some consider Jackson a sleepy place, but it has a lively and important history at the center of the gold rush. Many towns started as mining camps have faded into obscurity, but Jackson got a foothold and kept growing. Today the population is approaching 5,000, but plans are afoot for more housing and commercial development; it won't be a small town forever. Here is Main Street pictured at midnight, c. 1935, when most of the original two-story buildings still stood. (Courtesy Amador County Archives.)

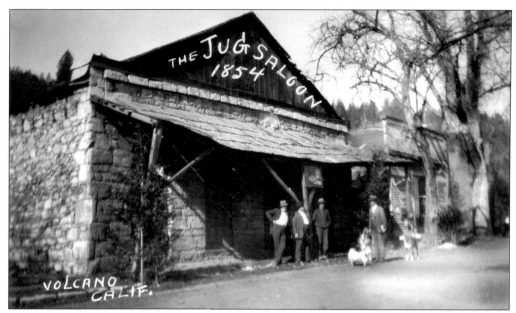

Volcano was a thriving place for many years due to gold mining. A number of saloons graced the town's streets, including the Jug, built in 1854 but pictured here c. 1920. (Courtesy Amador County Archives.)

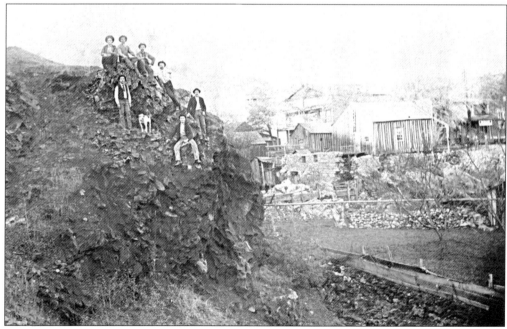

A group of Volcano men congregate on a large rock outcropping around 1905. The man in the center, leaning against the rock and wearing a white shirt, is Jim Grillo, son of a gold-rush Italian emigrant and one of the early Volcano residents, whose family has lived in Volcano for generations. This outcropping now overlooks the park on Main Street and is used to hold the manger scene at Christmastime. (Courtesy Terry Grillo.)

Plymouth, located near the northern boundary of Amador, had many businesses providing services and supplies to the local miners. Here is the Central Hotel pictured around 1898. (Courtesy Amador County Archives.)

Like Anwar Sadat and Franz Ferdinand, Amadoreans have always loved a parade. Here at the Horrible Parade, held on July 4, 1929, a somewhat disturbing Goddess of Liberty rides on a float on a transfer truck, observing and ostensibly judging all. The truck's driver is Lideo Valvo, and the building in the background belonged to the Piccardo family, who operated the Piccardo Brothers transfer service. Present-day Piccardo Way is at this location next to Jackson Gate Road. Little is known of the Horrible Parade today, but it was apparently an alternative to the more mainstream Fourth of July events seen elsewhere in this tome. An item from the *Sacramento Record Union* notes that a group calling itself "The Horribles" initiated the parade idea on June 11, 1891. (Courtesy Amador County Archives.)

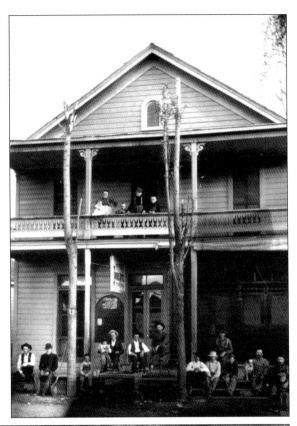

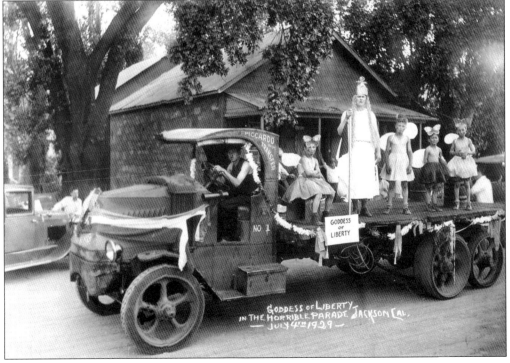

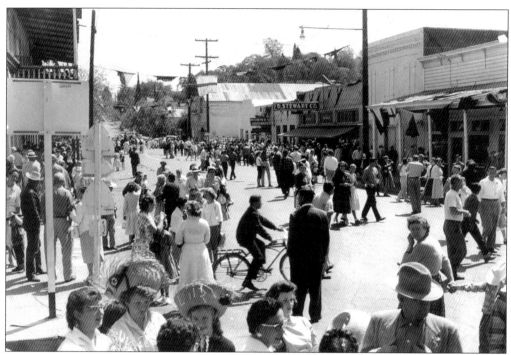

Civic events always bring people out in Amador. This was the annual Ione Homecoming held in Ione in the mid-1950s. (Courtesy City of Ione.)

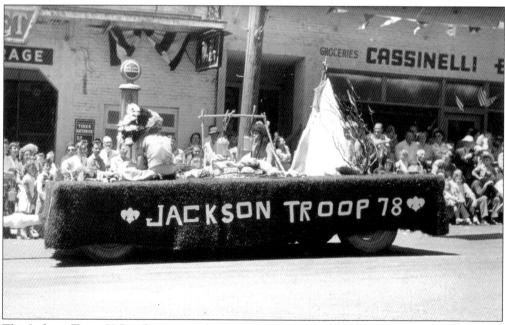

This Jackson Troop 78 Boy Scouts parade float, pictured in the 1952 Kit Carson Days parade, had a mixed Native American/Boy Scout message of tents, humanitarianism, and correct placement of cooking utensils. (Courtesy Amador County Archives.)

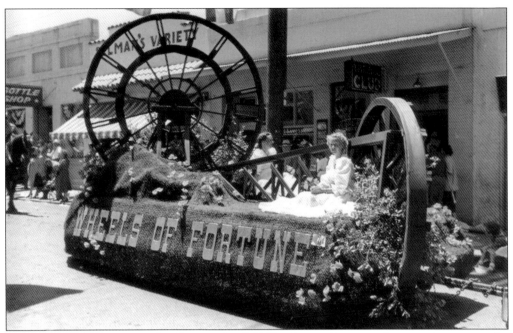

The "wheels of fortune" on this float in the 1952 Kit Carson Days parade are an homage to the tailing wheels formerly used by the Kennedy Mine north of Jackson. Those wheels, more than 50 feet in diameter, were used in mining operations for many years, starting in 1914, to lift mine waste in slurry form away from the mines and into a settling pond. Today they live on at the Kennedy Tailing Wheels Park. (Courtesy Amador County Archives.)

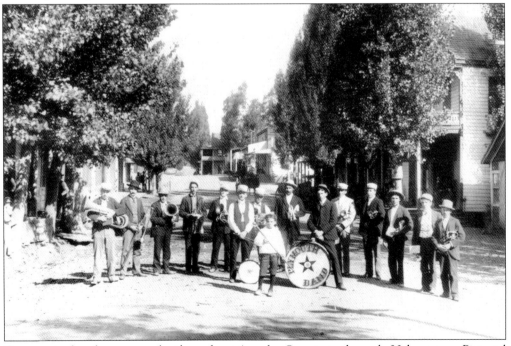

Community bands were popular throughout Amador County in the early 20th century. Pictured here is the Plymouth Band around 1900. (Courtesy Amador County Archives.)

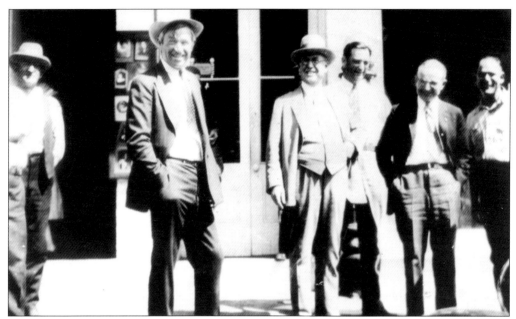

Noted cowboy humorist and quipper Will Rogers, originator of such quotes as "an onion can make people cry but there's never been a vegetable that can make people laugh" and "be thankful we're not getting all the government we're paying for," visited Amador County in September 1920 and is pictured here (second from left) along Main Street. To the right of Rogers, wearing glasses, is banker Charlis Culbert. Rogers filmed the zany comedy *Boys will Be Boys* in Jackson in 1920. (Courtesy Amador County Archives.)

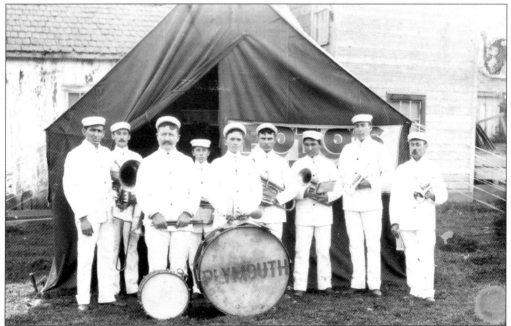

This is another community band from Plymouth, posing by a "foto" tent and distinguished from the one pictured on page 15 by its members' decidedly snappy uniforms. (Courtesy Amador County Archives.)

Kit Carson, for whom Highway 88's Carson Pass is named, was an impressive specimen of the "mountain man" genre and was famed for helping John C. Fremont map the western trails to the Pacific Ocean. For many years, the county has celebrated the exploits of this intrepid explorer and fur trapper, as evidenced by this 1966 advertisement. Among the events scheduled were the "quick draw" contest (and the undoubtedly harrowing finals held the second day), the self-explanatory beard contest, and the curious "mountain man hut." (Courtesy Amador County Archives.)

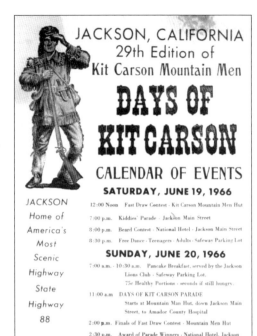

JACKSON, CALIFORNIA
29th Edition of
Kit Carson Mountain Men

DAYS OF
KIT CARSON

CALENDAR OF EVENTS

SATURDAY, JUNE 19, 1966

JACKSON

Home of

America's

Most

Scenic

Highway

State

Highway

88

12:00 Noon   Fast Draw Contest - Kit Carson Mountain Men Hut

7:00 p.m.   Kiddies' Parade - Jackson Main Street

8:00 p.m.   Beard Contest - National Hotel - Jackson Main Street

8:30 p.m.   Free Dance - Teenagers - Adults - Safeway Parking Lot

SUNDAY, JUNE 20, 1966

7:00 a.m. - 10:30 a.m.   Pancake Breakfast, served by the Jackson
              Lions Club - Safeway Parking Lot.
              75c Healthy Portions - seconds if still hungry.

11:00 a.m   DAYS OF KIT CARSON PARADE
              Starts at Mountain Man Hut, down Jackson Main
              Street, to Amador County Hospital

2:00 p.m.   Finals of Fast Draw Contest - Mountain Men Hut

2:30 p.m.   Award of Parade Winners - National Hotel, Jackson

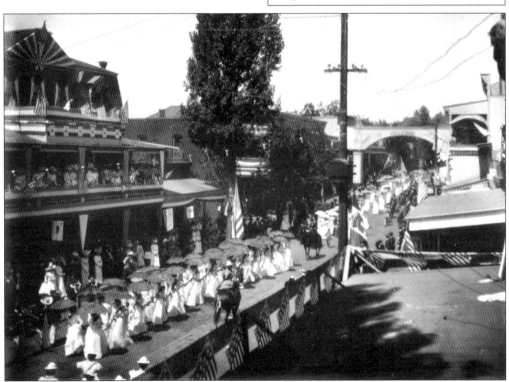

Sutter Creek's Main Street has long been a favorite Fourth of July parade locale, and the town continues having old-fashioned Fourth celebrations to this day. This c. 1900 parade seems to feature a precision marching parasol drill team that is possibly a division of the local Women's Christian Temperance Union. (Courtesy Amador County Archives.)

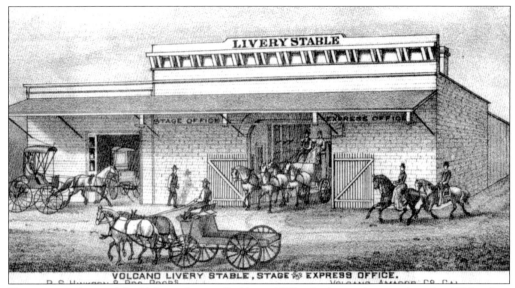

Here is an etching of the Volcano Livery Stable, *c.* 1870, which was destroyed in the 1920s when plans were made to flood the valley in which Volcano lies for a reservoir. This large brick stable sat where the post office is now located. (Courtesy Amador County Archives.)

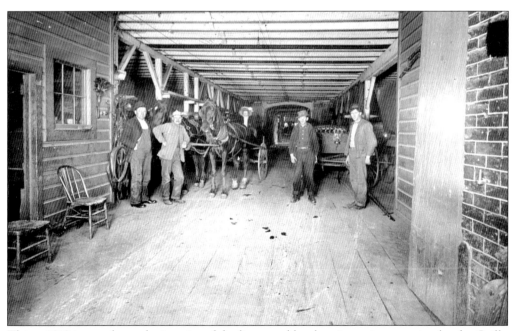

This *c.* 1910 image shows the interior of the livery stable when it was in operation by the Grillo Brothers. Pictured, from left to right, are Jim Grillo, Dominic Grillo, Sadie Gillick Grillo, unidentified, and Abe White. (Courtesy Amador County Archives.)

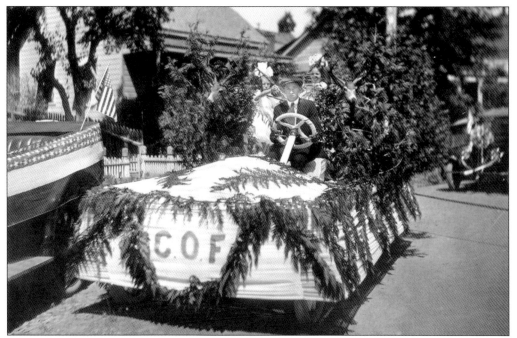

This is the Catholic Order of Foresters float in an undated parade in Jackson. (Courtesy Amador County Archives.)

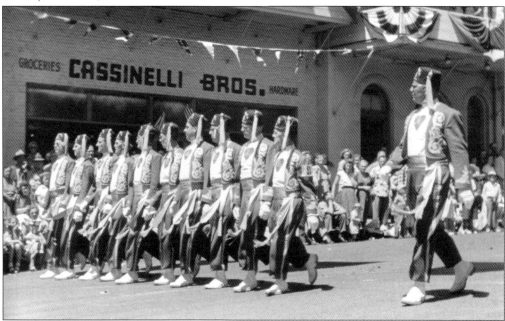

The 1952 Days of Kit Carson parade featured this impressive group from the Ancient Arabic Order of the Nobles of the Mystic Shrine, more commonly known as the Shriners. Note the relatively ornate fezzes, white gloves and shoes, and military precision of the marchers. This patrol appears to be in an "eyes right" presentation, which is typically done to recognize a dignitary or person of honor in the audience. The Cassinelli Brothers store in the background was the birthplace of winemaker Ernesto Gallo. (Courtesy Amador County Archives.)

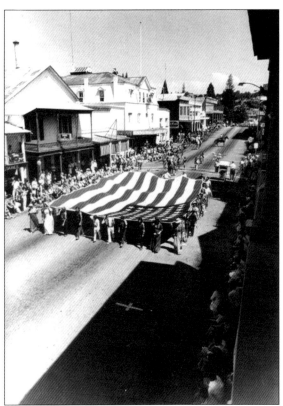

They don't come much bigger than this specimen of Old Glory, held aloft in a Fourth of July parade in Sutter Creek, probably the 1976 bicentennial celebration. It was most likely being carried by members of the Native Sons of the Golden West. (Courtesy Amador County Archives.)

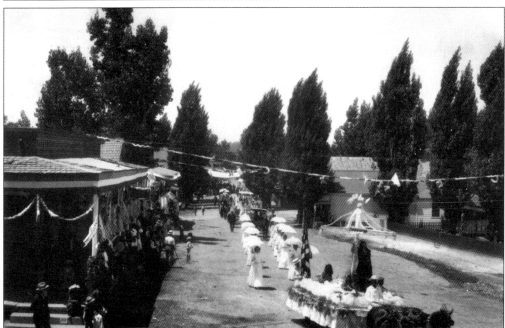

Another parade of white-dressed women, led by an ornate horse-drawn float, wends its way up Plymouth's Main Street during a Fourth of July parade, c. 1900. (Courtesy Amador County Archives.)

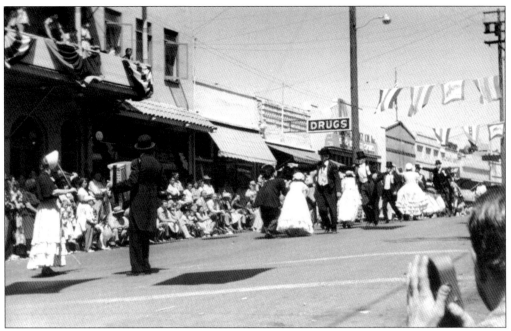

It seems like a difficult trick, but that didn't stop this group from square dancing down Jackson's Main Street in this 1952 parade during Kit Carson Days. (Courtesy Amador County Archives.)

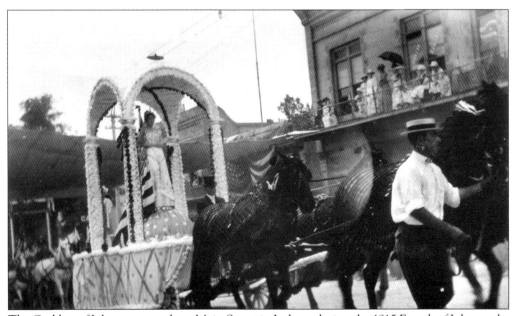

The Goddess of Liberty proceeds up Main Street in Jackson during the 1915 Fourth of July parade. In the background is the Webb building; Richard Webb was an early landowner and owner of the *Amador Ledger* newspaper. (Courtesy Amador County Archives.)

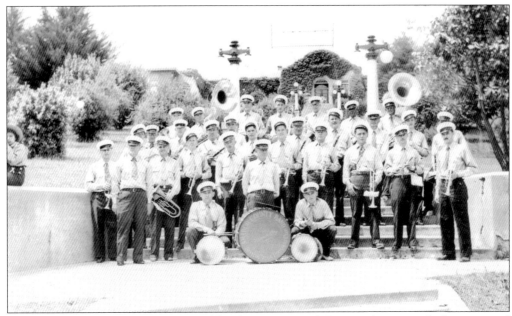

The Amador County Band (sponsored by the Sutter Creek Boosters) poses in Jackson around 1940. The Boosters were formed in the late 1930s. (Courtesy Amador County Archives.)

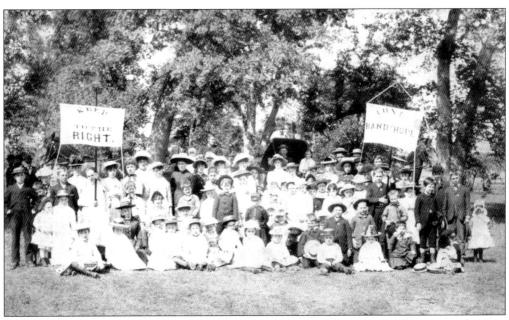

The Ione "Band of Hope," a sort of children's temperance union based upon others created in San Joaquin County in the mid-1800s, poses for a photograph in 1899. These groups got their start in Britain in 1847; they taught working-class children "the evils of drink." Many such bands had choirs that sang inspirational songs against sin and drinking. In the gold country, there was a fair amount of temperance efforts due to the excessive alcohol consumption of many citizens and subsequent damage to communities. The cautionary sign reading, "Keep to the Right," however, is actually on the left. (Courtesy Amador County Archives.)

Lake Amador, a man-made lake, opened in 1968 east of Ione, near Lake Camanche. This advertisement from that same year touts the fishing opportunities, with the lake having been stocked with 50,000 fish at the time. Today it is still stocked regularly with fish and is a favored spot for bass, trout, and catfish. In 1969, the lake was the site of the Gold Rush music festival (see pages 44–46). (Courtesy Amador County Archives.)

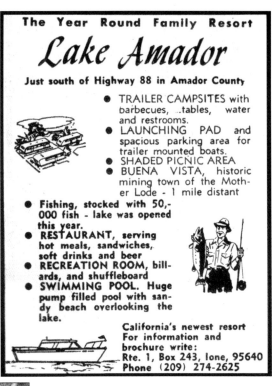

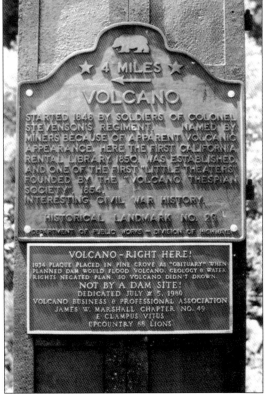

These plaques in Volcano commemorate the history of the town and show off the humor of E Clampus Vitus, a history and drinking society active throughout the foothills and California, who appended the 1934 historical landmark plaque at the top with the more whimsical one at the bottom in 1980. It explains that Volcano survived despite a planned dam that would have flooded the town; ergo "Volcano didn't drown—not by a dam site!" The upper plaque was located originally in Pine Grove as a "memorial" to the now not-flooded Volcano. (Courtesy Amador County Archives.)

23

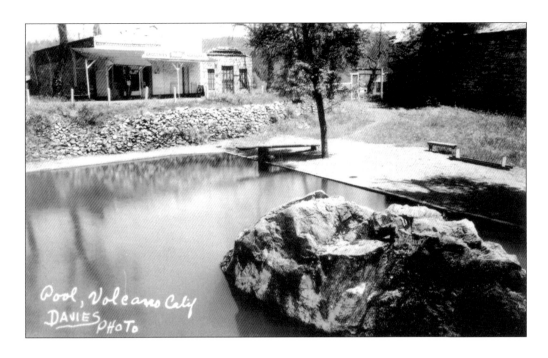

From the 1930s to the late 1970s, Volcano sported this lovely swimming pool west of Main Street. It was fed by water diverted from Sutter Creek and provided a welcome respite from hot summer weather for many a Volcano youth. However, one local resident simply remembers, "It was cold!" The rock in the middle can be seen clearly in the park today sans water. (Courtesy Amador County Archives.)

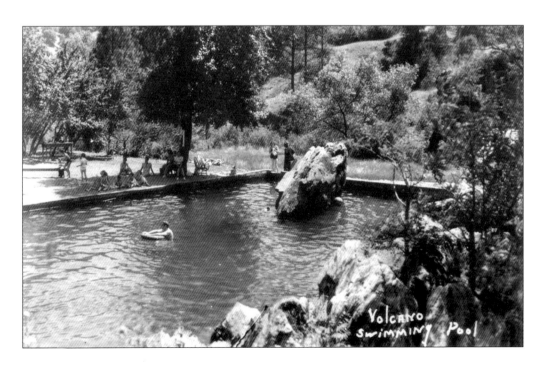

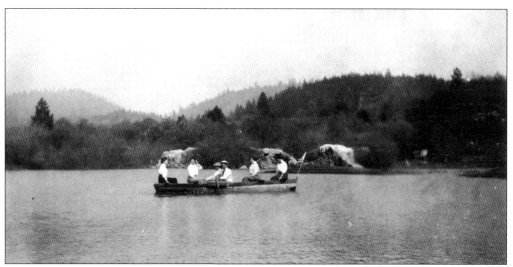

Also in the early part of the century, a dam on Sutter Creek created a short-lived lake called Lake Volcano, which provided a picturesque spot for boating, seen here in this *c.* 1910 photograph. (Courtesy Amador County Archives.)

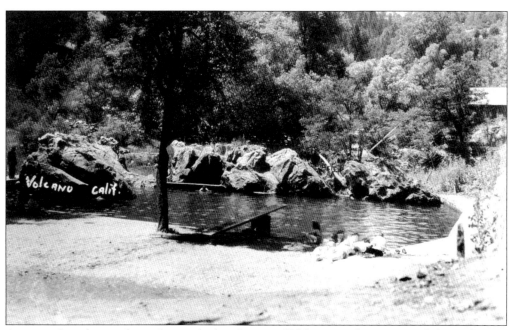

A group of youths sun themselves at the late, lamented Volcano pool, conveniently located across the street from Poggio's general store. (Courtesy Amador County Archives.)

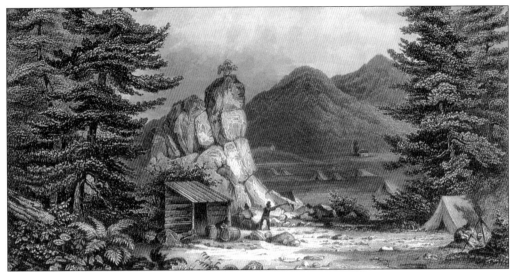

This *c.* 1849 etching of early Volcano entitled *The Volcano Golddiggings* shows an early view of the settlement by artist Bayard Taylor. It first appeared in his book *El Dorado, or Adventures in the Path of Empire.* The landscape around the town changed dramatically due to hydraulic gold mining in the late 1800s. Miners actually named the town Volcano because it looked like it sat in a volcanic caldera. The area depicted behind the shack is the Masonic Cave Area. (Courtesy Laurie Hedger.)

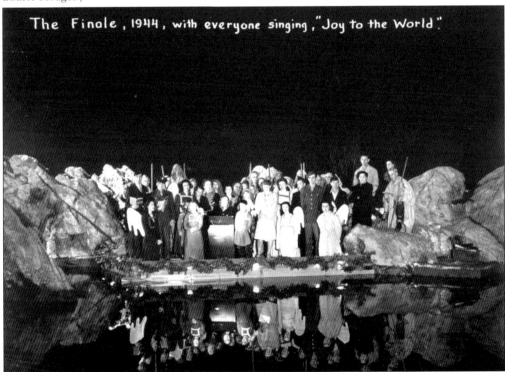

This card from December 1944 shows Volcano residents at a Christmas Eve celebration at the town pool near Main and Consolation Streets. Luckily for the town, all of its fighting men came home safely from World War II the following year. (Courtesy Terry Grillo.)

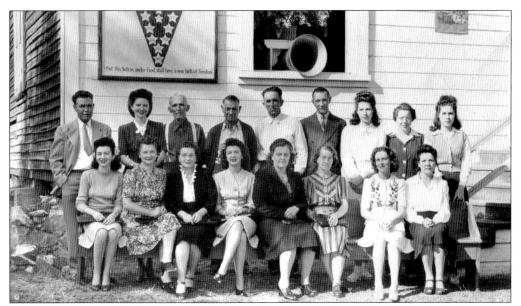

Volcano-area residents in the c. 1941 Volcano Roll of Honor, from left to right, included (first row) Nellie Cook Dower, Goldie Porter, Mayme Giannini, Bertha Bonneau, Betty Cook, Irene Cook, Mabel Brockman, and Marjorie Cook; (second row) Charles Brockman, Barbara Cook, Emmett Gillick, Pete Barone, Robert Porter, Charles Cook, Lois Hale Bonneau, Evelyn Giannini, and Doris Hale Bonneau. (Courtesy Amador County Archives.)

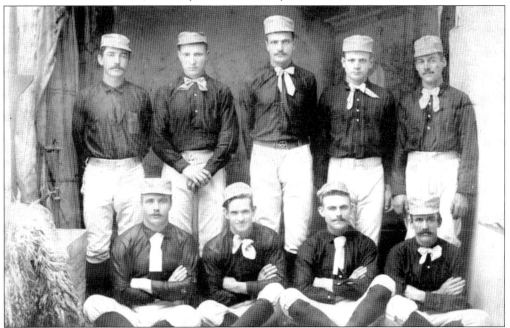

Baseball fever was all over the country in the 1890s, and Amador was no exception. Here is the Volcano baseball team, pictured during that decade. When the group traveled to games in far-off locales (like Sutter Creek), they were normally taunted by the hosting team's fans. To stave off the ridicule, their fans had a chant that went in part, "We are the boys who fear no noise, although we're far from home!" (Courtesy Terry Grillo.)

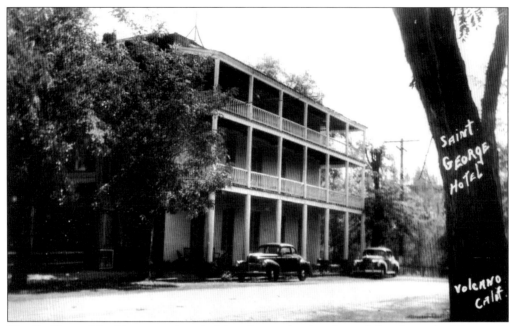

The St. George Hotel is among Amador's best-known landmarks, and the elegant building, with its sweeping balconies, is a popular spot for weddings and other celebrations. The hotel was built in late 1863 (at the site of the former Eureka and Empire Hotels, both of which burned down) with 14-inch-thick masonry walls to "thwart the demonic Fire Dragon" as builder B. F. George so succinctly said. Here the hotel is pictured around 1935. (Courtesy Amador County Archives.)

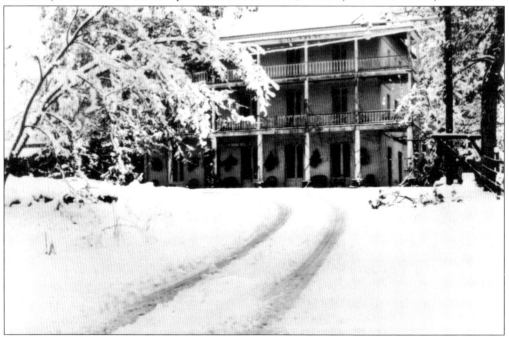

The St. George, pictured here c. 1932, is the first building one sees when driving into Volcano. The elegant colonnettes, wooden balustrades, and French doors opening to the balconies make it a beautiful sight in sunny or snowy weather. (Courtesy Amador County Archives.)

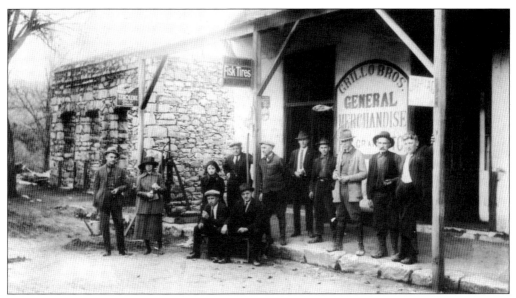

A group gathers at the Grillo Brothers store in Volcano around 1931, when plans were afoot to flood the city for a reservoir. Pictured, from left to right, are (standing) Otto Strohlberg (AP correspondent), Pearl White (reporter from the *Amador Dispatch*), Eileen Grillo, "Dutch" Boro, Harvey Mason, Sam Minadeux, Lee Gardner, Bill Daniels, John Canvin, and Jim Grillo; (seated) Frank Cuneo and Bill Tam. (Courtesy Terry Grillo.)

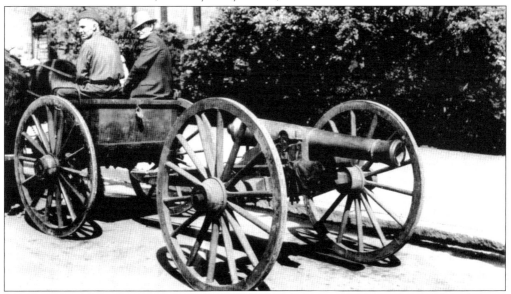

"Old Abe," also called the Volcano Blues Cannon, is the name of a cannon with a long history. Pictured here *c.* 1925, the cannon was supposedly brought to Amador covertly (in a hearse) in 1862 by Yankee sympathizers called the Volcano Blues during the Civil War. Salvaged from an abandoned sailing ship in San Francisco, it is sometimes called the Blues cannon, given its heritage. Ostensibly the idea was to quash any possibilities of a Confederate uprising in the gold country, but no shots were ever fired in anger. The cannon, however, has traveled now and again to various festivals and reenactments, where it does what a cannon is made to do. Built in 1837, it is the oldest six-pound bronze cannon in the United States. (Courtesy Amador County Archives.)

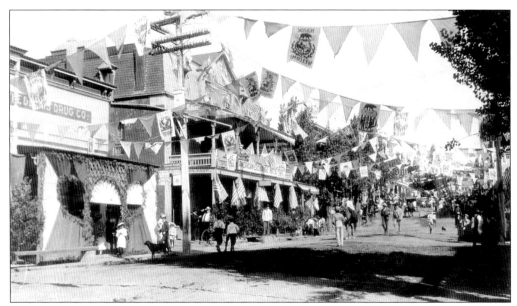

Preparations for the Fourth of July parade on Sutter Creek's Main Street in 1906 included colorful bunting, copious flags, and a banner reading "Welcome NSGW." That acronym is for the popular fraternal organization Native Sons of the Golden West, of course. (Courtesy Amador County Archives.)

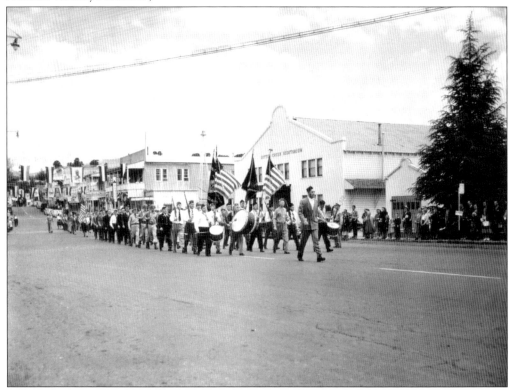

This is a more modern Fourth of July parade in Sutter Creek, around 1950. Leading the parade is World War II veteran Don Vicini. (Courtesy Amador County Archives.)

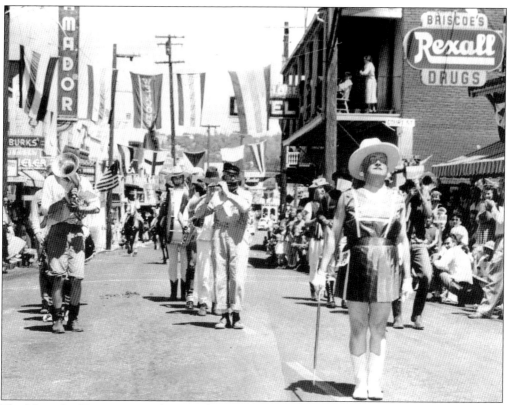

The Hamador Histerics, seen here at the Kit Carson Days parade in Jackson on June 19, 1955, were a curious marching band, wherein the participants dressed somewhat differently than more formal marching bands. The leader, in front, was drum "majorette" Basilio "Dolly" Ricci, who ran a barbershop on Jackson's Main Street for many years and his son Gino still does as of this writing. (Courtesy Amador County Archives.)

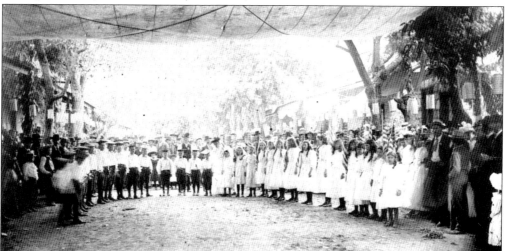

This elegantly dressed group posed on Volcano's Main Street for a Fourth of July celebration around 1880. The buildings on the right side are the present-day Cobblestone Theatre and the Country Store. (Courtesy Terry Grillo.)

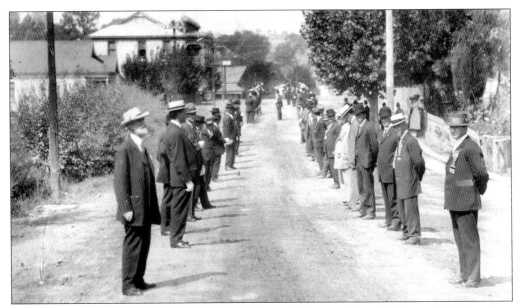

Mourners line up along a funeral route on Broadway in Jackson in this *c.* 1915 image. The Broadway Hotel is in the background. The man at left is George Gordon, a prominent school official and the son of Marvin Gordon, Jackson's first city judge. (Courtesy Amador County Archives.)

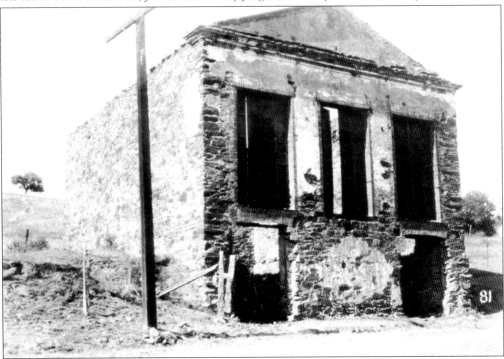

The old Butte City store still remains on the east side of Highway 49 south of Jackson, looking similar to this 1934 photograph. The building was first run by Xavier Benoist as a store and bakery starting in 1857 before Enrico Ginocchio took over. For a time in the late 1800s, the settlement of Butte City rivaled Jackson in activity and population. The store's walls, made of Calaveras schist fieldstone, have withstood the test of time very well. (Courtesy Amador County Archives.)

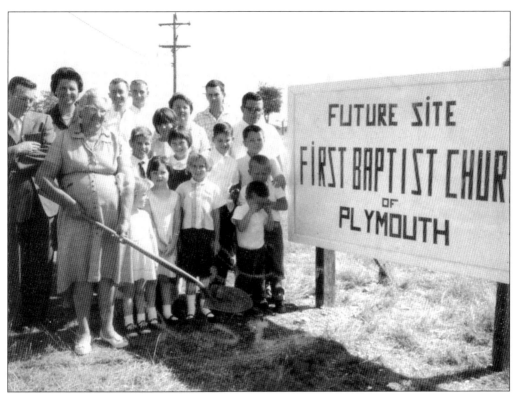

Plymouth citizens of the 1950s pose during the groundbreaking of the First Baptist Church. (Courtesy Amador County Archives.)

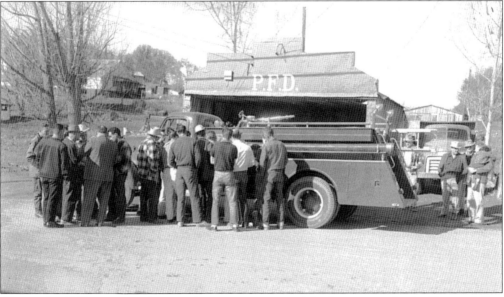

Also in the 1950s, a group of men gather to inspect one of the fire engines for the Plymouth Fire Department outside of the firehouse, which ironically burned down a few years later. The man in the white hat, third from right, is the late John Begovich. He was a city supervisor, state senator, and World War II hero. (Courtesy Amador County Archives.)

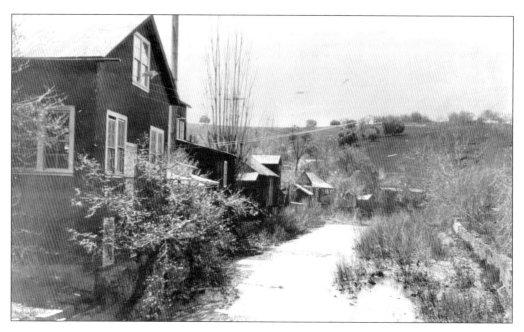

The bridge over Sutter Creek has long been a favorite spot to gaze out at the creek and the hills toward Volcano. Here is the same view around 1900 (above) and in 2005 (below). The building at left housed a steam laundry in 1900 and a car dealer in 2005. How times have changed . . . (Above courtesy Amador County Archives; below courtesy author.)

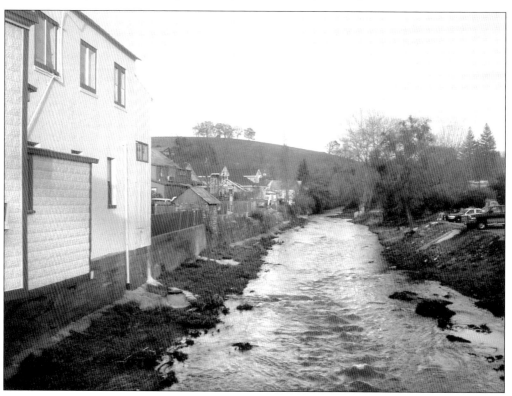

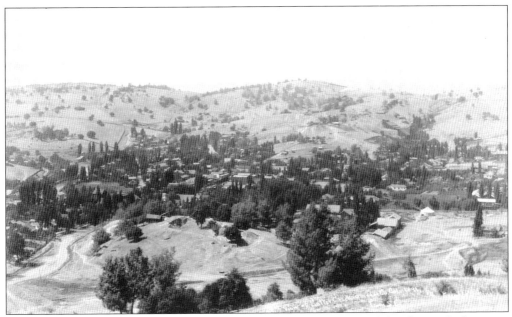

Sutter Creek, pictured here from a nearby hilltop in 1891, is named for the creek that runs through it, which in turn is named for John Sutter. Sutter is the celebrated Californian who was instrumental in the gold rush after the discovery of sought-after metal at his mill on the American River at Coloma. The town was an important supply center for the mining industry. (Courtesy Amador County Archives.)

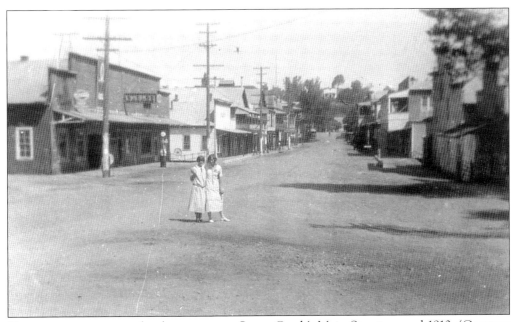

Two young women pose for the camera on Sutter Creek's Main Street around 1910. (Courtesy Amador County Archives.)

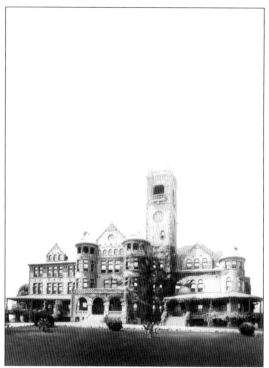

Easily Ione's most impressive structure, if not all of Amador's, Preston Castle was erected in 1894. Also referred to as the Preston School of Industry (which still exists nearby), it housed youths that had been referred there by the court system—what today might be termed "juvenile delinquents." The Romanesque Revival castle was a "reform school" and rehabilitation center for these youths, who were expected to learn good living habits through hard work and discipline. The first seven youths arrived in 1894 as wards of the court transferred from San Quentin prison in the San Francisco area. Today the castle is in poor condition and not open to the public except for occasional tours, but the Preston Castle Foundation (www.prestoncastle.com) is working to restore it to its former glory. It is listed both as a California Historic Landmark and on the National Register of Historic Places. (Courtesy Amador County Archives.)

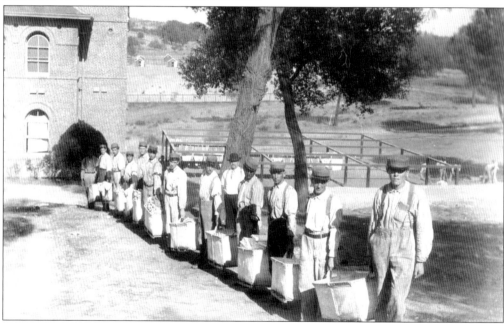

Cadets, or wards, at the Preston Castle were given demanding yet structured tasks to help them rebuild their troubled lives. Part of the impetus for the reform-school movement was that in earlier times, housing juvenile offenders among adult prisoners often led to abusive situations. No penal system can be called perfect, but it was places like Preston that sought to establish a separate judicial and correctional system specifically for juveniles. One former ward was country-western singer Merle Haggard. This photograph was taken c. 1899. (Courtesy Amador County Archives.)

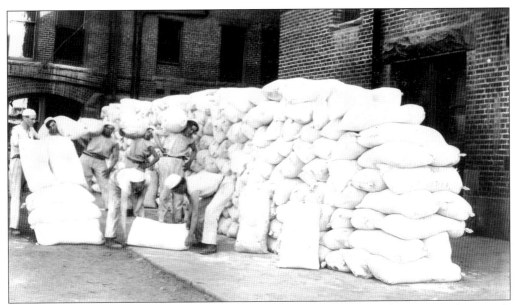

Hard manual labor was a daily task for most of the wards at Preston, as this c. 1900 photograph demonstrates. Preston is unused today, but the Preston School of Industry still exists as a juvenile detention facility nearby. Ione also has Mule Creek State Prison, an adult detention facility with over 3,000 inmates, including, at one point, rap mogul "Suge" Knight. (Courtesy Amador County Archives.)

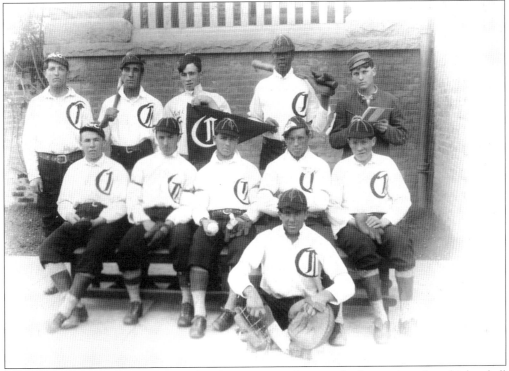

It was not all fun and games at Preston, but there was some diversion for the wards, such as this baseball team, simply known as the Preston Baseball Team. (Courtesy Amador County Archives.)

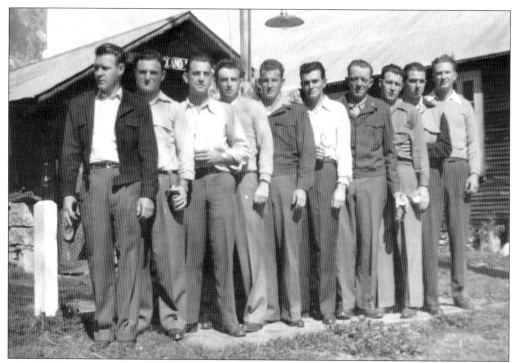

Here are some of Volcano's World War II–era servicemen, seen at Christmastime 1945. Pictured, from left to right, are Arnold Jonas, Bob Richards, Gene Barone, Charles Cook, Jim "Sonny" Giannini, Lester Cook, Kenneth Jonas, Clarence Barone, Charles Bonneau, and Willard Bonneau. The boys are standing in front of the "Old Abe" cannon, and most appear to be enjoying a refreshing beverage. (Courtesy Amador County Archives.)

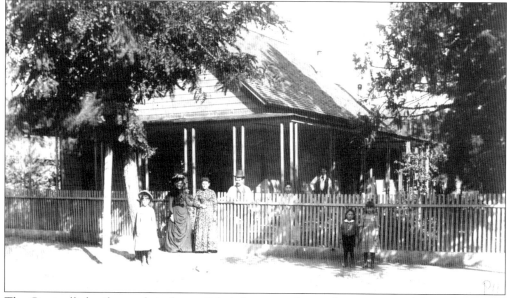

The Cassinelli family stands in front of their home on the southeast corner of Consolation and Plug Streets in Volcano around 1895. Their original home at the same spot burned down in 1888. (Courtesy Terry Grillo.)

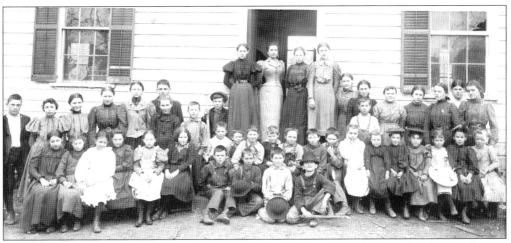

A group of students and teachers pose in front of the one-room Volcano School around 1898. (Courtesy Terry Grillo.)

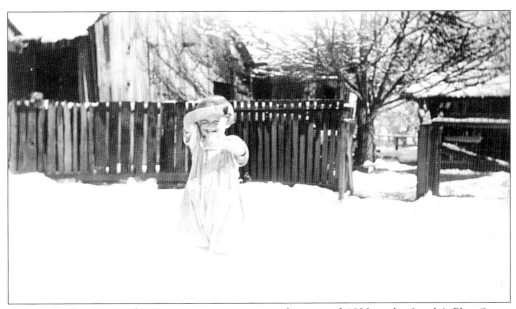

Wilson Grillo plays in the snow on a sunny winter day around 1920 at the family's Plug Street home. (Courtesy Terry Grillo.)

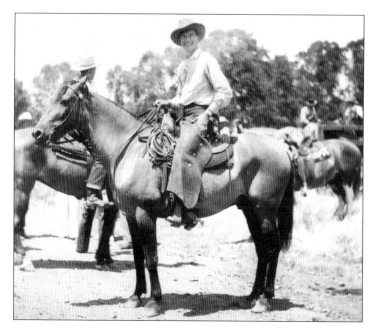

Dave Brubeck, the famed jazz pianist who recorded the huge hit "Take 5" in 1959 on his *Time Out* record, was born in Contra Costa County but grew up in Ione on a farm. He played in various dance bands around Amador during the 1930s. He made the cover of *Time* magazine in 1954 and has toured the world extensively playing his fine brand of cool jazz. Here he is astride a horse during a cattle drive in 1936. Note the long fingers—those are for keyboards, not cattle! (Courtesy Brubeck family.)

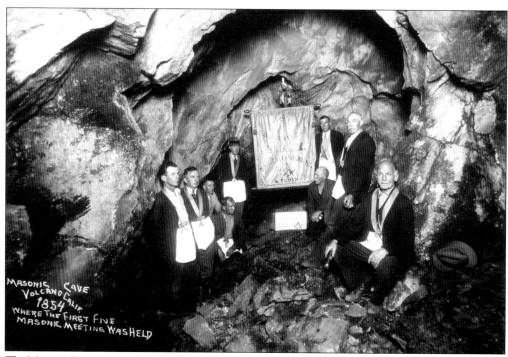

The Masonic Caves, just outside of Volcano, were where the pre-charter Masons held their first five meetings, starting in 1854, before a more substantial lodge was built. (Courtesy Amador County Archives.)

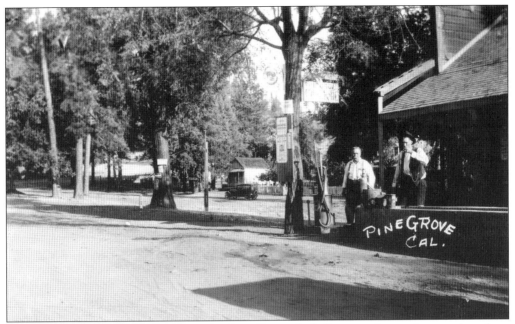

This real photograph postcard shows the Pine Grove Cash Store market and gas station along Highway 88 in Pine Grove, *c.* 1932. (Courtesy Amador County Archives.)

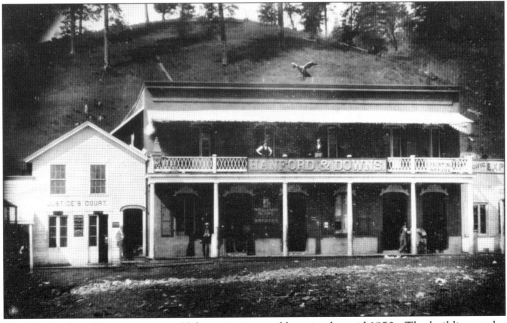

The Hanford and Downs store in Volcano is pictured here in the mid-1850s. The building at the time housed the Wells Fargo office and the post office. To the left is the Justice's Court, which meted out frontier justice to ne'er-do-wells. This store burned down in the late 1870s. Hanford and Downs also had stores in Jackson and Sutter Creek. (Courtesy Amador County Archives.)

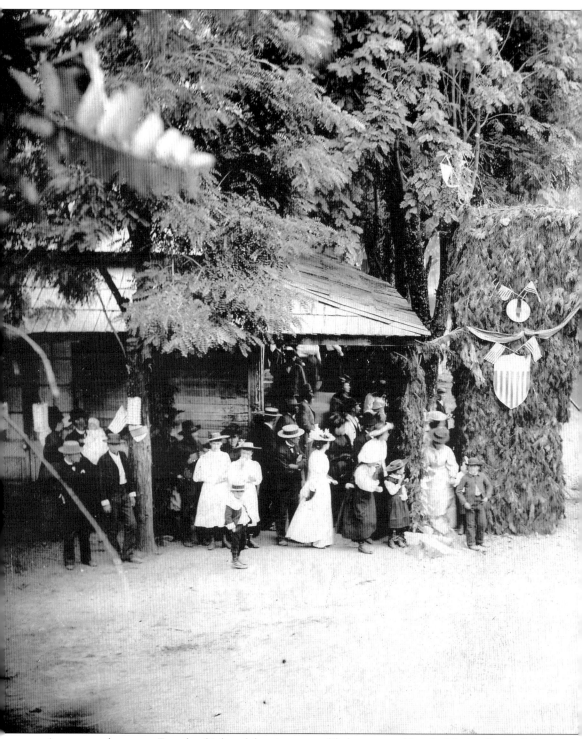

An extremely ornate Fourth of July celebration, most likely arranged by the Native Sons of the Golden West, brings horse-drawn floats into the center of Volcano at the corner of Main and Consolation Streets in this *c.* 1870 image. Some of the people standing in the shadows below

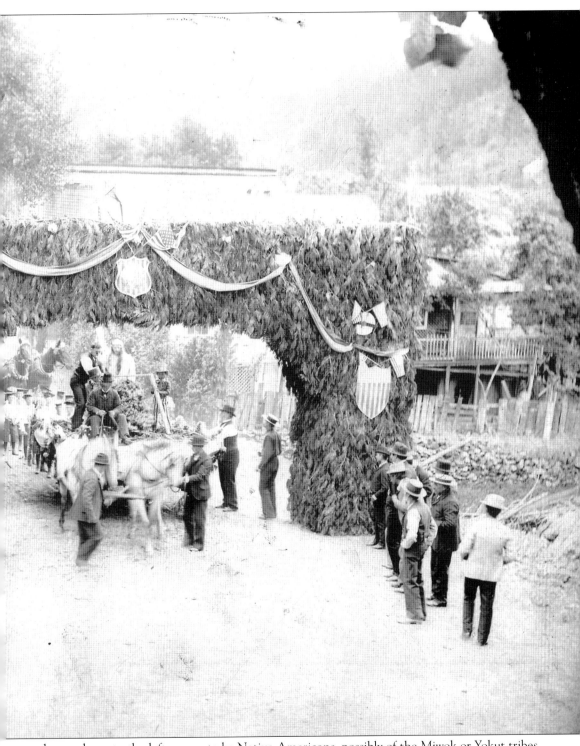

the overhang to the left appear to be Native Americans, possibly of the Miwok or Yokut tribes. (Courtesy Amador County Archives.)

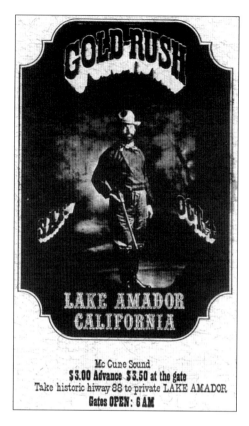

The Age of Aquarius came to Lake Amador on October 4, 1969, when the Gold Rush Festival brought with it approximately 50,000 music fans. This miniature Woodstock featured top acts Santana, Taj Mahal, Bo Diddley, Albert Collins (also known as "the Master of the Telecaster"), Kaliedoscope, Al Wilson, Southwind, Ike and Tina Turner, Sons of Champlin, Country Weather, Cold Blood, John Fahey, Linn County, and Southwind. Local officials were stunned by the huge turnout, and while there was some consternation over the hippies' worldview and drug use, the event was a peaceful one. (Courtesy Amador County Archives.)

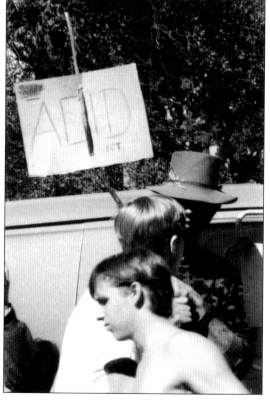

This image depicts what some locals were concerned about—the apparently open dealing of controlled substances at the festival. And while a Volkswagen van sporting a cardboard sign that reads "ACID" in the middle of a 1960s rock concert doesn't necessarily mean it's any specific kind of acid, it seems a safe bet it wasn't muriatic. (Courtesy Amador County Archives.)

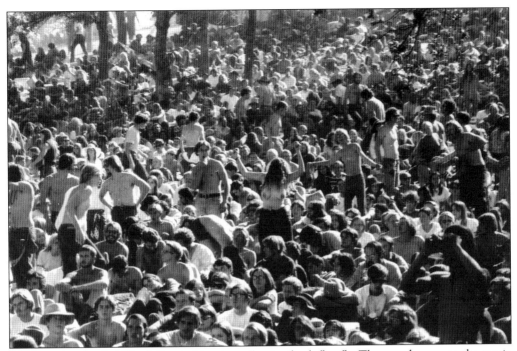

The crowd at the Gold Rush Festival lets its collective freak flag fly. Thousands came to the music festival from all around the West. (Courtesy Amador County Archives.)

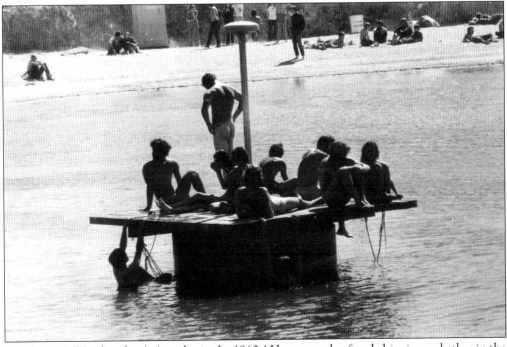

No, this isn't Woodstock, it's Amador in the 1960s! Here a gaggle of nude hippies sunbathes in the swimming pond at Lake Amador during the festival. (Courtesy Amador County Archives.)

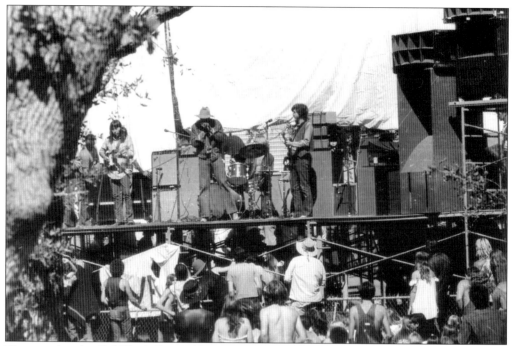

The crowd at the Gold Rush Festival listens attentively to legendary bluesman Taj Mahal on the main stage. (Courtesy Amador County Archives.)

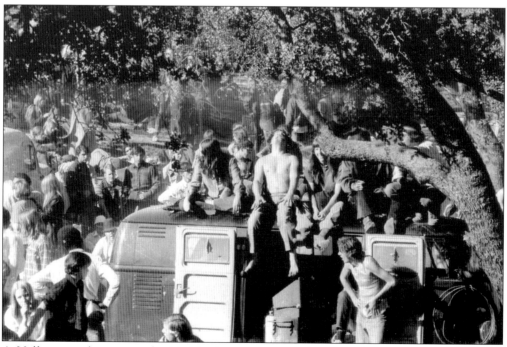

A Volkswagen bus covered with hippies was among the myriad attractions of the Gold Rush Festival.

Nitro-burnin' rockabilly wizard Brian Setzer is among the big-name entertainers to grace the Jackson Rancheria's Margaret P. Dalton Pavilion stage in recent years; his Brian Setzer Orchestra Christmas Extravaganza tour in 2005 packed the 2,000-seat venue. The Rancheria has grown from humble beginnings in a roadside Quonset hut to a major entertainment and gaming venue. With the rise of Indian gaming throughout California, the Jackson Rancheria band of Miwok Indians has profited handsomely but also continually invests back into the resort. Most people view the development favorably, although residents of Ridge Road have ongoing headaches with speeding cars going to and from the casino. The Rancheria is now a major employer in the Amador region and a prime spot to see nationally touring entertainers. (Photograph by Tommy Maguire.)

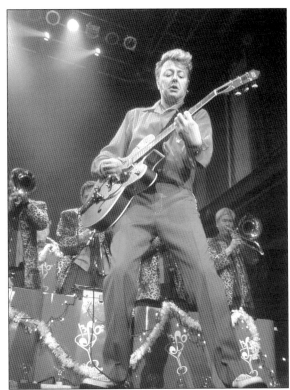

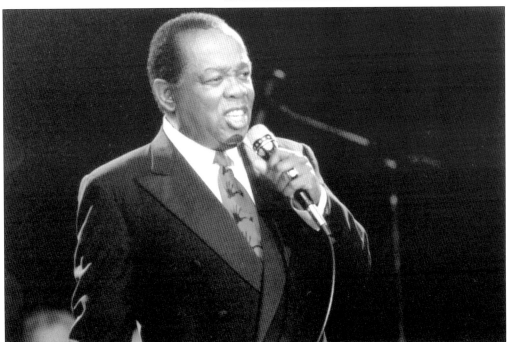

You'll never find another singer like the late, great Lou Rawls, but the Jackson Rancheria was lucky enough to have him grace its stage. Lou's honey-smooth voice thrilled concertgoers at the Rancheria a few years before his untimely passing at age 70 in 2006. (Courtesy Jackson Rancheria.)

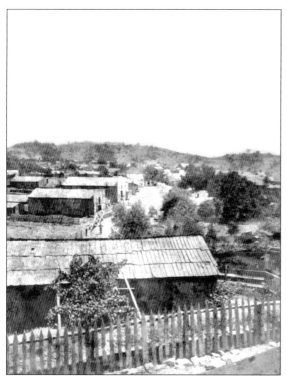

Drytown never got to be very big, although the hills around this tiny hamlet on Highway 49 teemed with miners during the gold rush. The town is said to be the first established in Amador and had a fairly active mining industry, although it was mostly destroyed by fire in 1857. It was not "dry" in the alcoholic sense—there were plenty of saloons here once—but rather because of the dry landscape (the town, called Dry Diggins in the old days, sits on Arroyo Seco, or Dry Creek). At one time, William Randolph Hearst's father operated a printing shop and an office here, and George McManus, the creator of the long-lived comic strip *Bringing up Father*, had space here. Today the town is small and has a handful of shops and a gold rush-era theatre that is now an antiques collective. This is Drytown as it appeared in 1866; gold was first discovered here in Amador in 1848. (Courtesy Amador County Archives.)

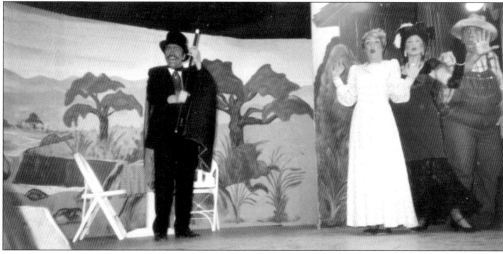

For almost 40 years, Drytown's small theater hosted the Claypipers, the longest-running melodrama group in California. Starting in 1958 with four families producing a show, the group was joined by others over the years, and several generations of families participated in the western-themed, old-time plays (replete with "Olios," or small vaudevillian side acts between set changes). Many of the participants were from the San Francisco peninsula, such as Duncan Fife of Foster City, pictured here with cape and dastardly moustache as "The Villian." Beside him at stage right in this 1980 production of *Dirty Work at the Crossroads* are, from left to right, Jan Crawford, Robin Sands Fife as "The Fallen Woman," and Ben Levine as "Mookie." Sadly, financing for the theatre fell apart, and the final play was in 1996. The theatre, known for many years as the Piper Playhouse, is now used for an antiques collective. (Courtesy Duncan Fife.)

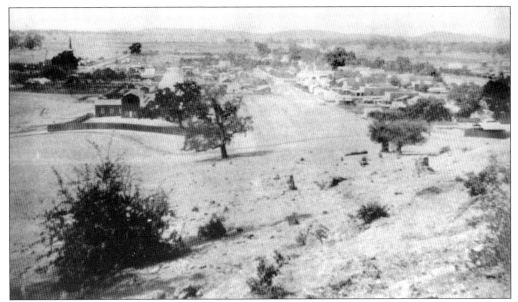

Ione, pictured here in 1866, remains a small country town despite the gradual encroachment of modern life. Unlike many gold-county hamlets, it continued to grow, albeit modestly, after the gold rush. The city was laid out in 1853 by Thomas B. Rickey and claims to be the largest town in Amador, but that's probably because they're counting the thousands of inmates at Mule Creek State Prison and Preston School of Industry along with the voluntary residents. (Courtesy Amador County Archives.)

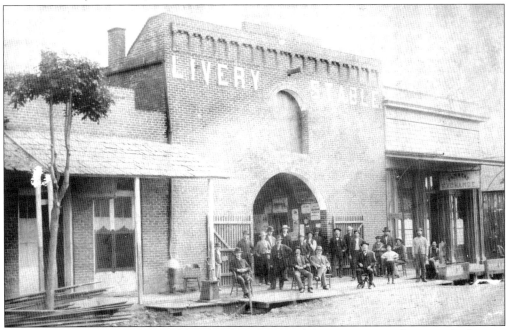

Pictured here is Ione's Livery Stable around 1899. As with many towns at the time, the liveries became a default social hub, as transportation was dependent on horses. Ione's place on a rail line (the Amador Central, Union Pacific, and successors) probably helped it to survive after the age of horses had passed. (Courtesy Amador County Archives.)

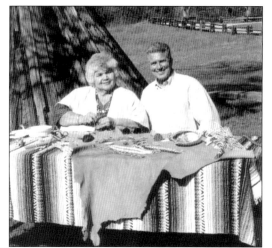

Amador has an extensive history of Native American culture and peoples, and there are many people of direct or partial Indian descent in the county today. Pictured here among native wares, c. 1994, are Amador resident and Miwok tribe member Ramona Dutschke and television host Huell Howser at the Chaw'se Indian Grinding Rock State Park near Pine Grove. Aside from the grinding rock area used in olden days to prepare food, the park's museum has basketry, feather regalia, jewelry, arrow points, and other tools on display. (Courtesy Amador County Archives.)

Foothills residents with Native American heritage pose at Chaw'se with television host Huell Howser, who in 1994 produced a show about the park. Pictured, from left to right, are Sarah Coran, Rita Nunes, Marcus Peters, Jen Denton, Huell Howser, Allen Walloupe, and David Snooks. (Courtesy Amador County Archives.)

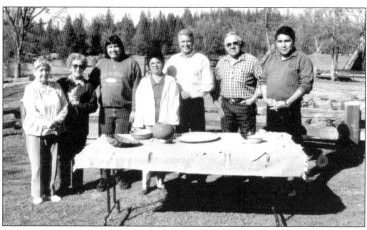

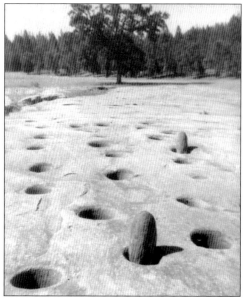

The Chaw'se Indian Grinding Rock State Park, located between Volcano and Pine Grove, has an extensive collection of Native American artifacts from throughout the foothill region, including Northern, Central, and Southern Miwok, Washo, Maidu, Monache, Konkow, Tubatulabal, Foothill Yokuts, and Nisenan. Pictured here around 1940 is the largest Indian grinding rock known in the country; it is 150 by 60 feet and pockmarked with hundreds of mortar holes. The native people used these rocks for centuries to grind acorns, berries, and grains. The park, which also has a traditional ceremonial roundhouse and a small campground, has several large rock outcroppings with 1,185 mortar holes all told. (Courtesy Amador County Archives.)

Two

MINES, MILLS, AND MACHINERY

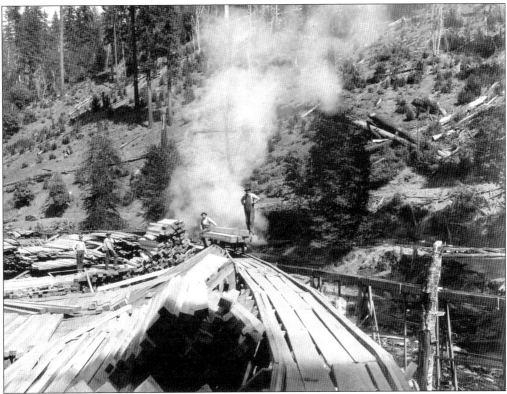

Amador's forested upcountry area, above Pine Grove, has large timber resources that for many years have provided lumber for various purposes. In this 1910 image, workers at a lumber mill in the Pioneer area above Tiger Creek process lumber for Pacific Gas and Electric Company's (PG&E) ambitious Mokelumne River Project—a series of four hydroelectric power plants along the river. In the old days, before they were cut down, pine trees grew as far down as Jackson. (Courtesy PG&E.)

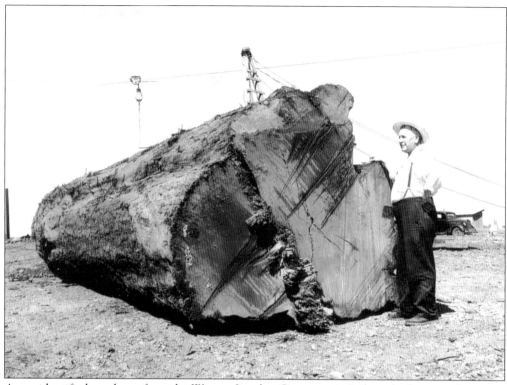

An unidentified employee from the Winton Lumber Company in Jackson looks over a huge tree segment before processing, c. 1952. (Courtesy Amador County Archives.)

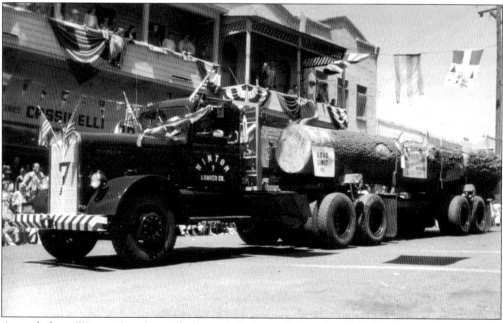

A truck from Winton Lumber rolls through Jackson during the 1952 Kit Carson Days parade, sporting what can only be described as some big wood. The sign in the middle reads, "Logged by Logger and Timber Workers Local 2873." (Courtesy Amador County Archives.)

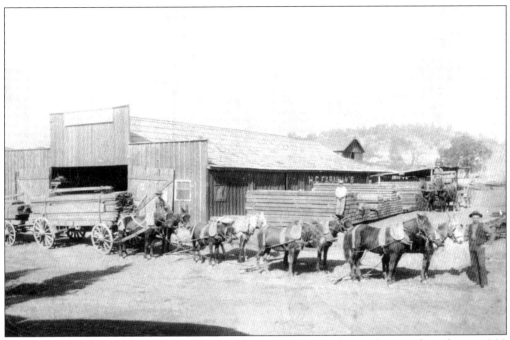

A team prepares to haul a load of lumber from the Plymouth Lumber Yard in this *c.* 1900 photograph. (Courtesy Amador County Archives.)

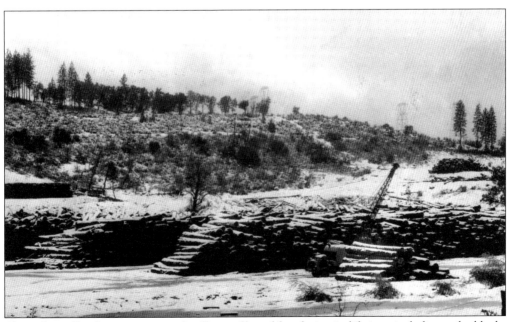

The cedar mill in Pioneer processed millions of board feet during its lifetime, including cedar blocks used for pencil manufacturing. In this 1964 photograph, snow covers logs awaiting processing at the mill. (Courtesy Amador County Archives.)

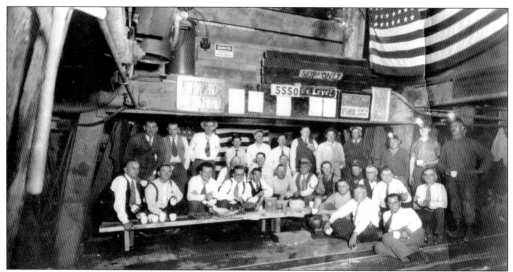

It can be difficult to get a good meal one mile underground but not for the Jackson Lions Club, pictured here c. 1930, as dinner guests of the Argonaut Mine in Jackson. Though the mine at the time went more than 6,100 feet deep, this group chose to eschew hubris and dine at the sensible 5,500-foot level. (Courtesy Amador County Archives.)

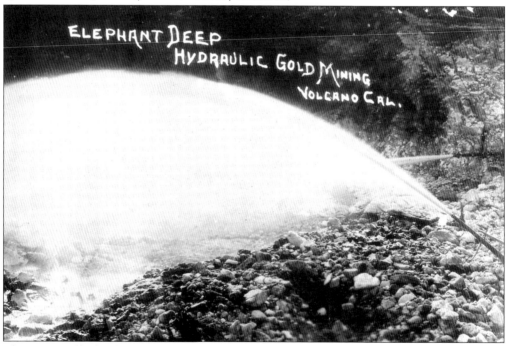

The process of hydraulic mining, wherein high-pressure water streams washed placer gold deposits out of loose dirt, did immeasurable damage to the earth throughout the gold country. It was a much more efficient way to search for gold than panning in streams, but washing away entire hillsides, as pictured here at the Elephant Deep Mine c. 1880, resulted in considerable downstream pollution from the silt and debris washing into rivers, not to mention the scarring of the land itself. The high-pressure nozzles on the water cannons were called "monitors;" two are visible in this photograph. (Courtesy Amador County Archives.)

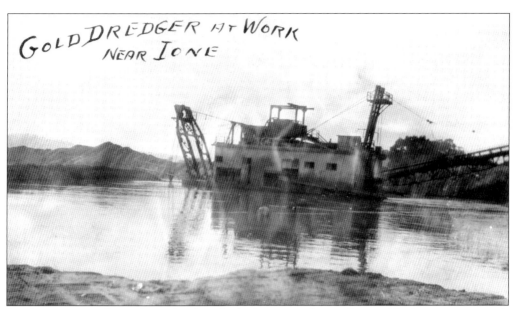

Dredging was another industrialized method of mining, wherein large cable-driven cranes, such as this one pictured in Ione in the 1880s, scooped up and sifted earth and mud from rivers, lakes, and ponds. (Courtesy Amador County Archives.)

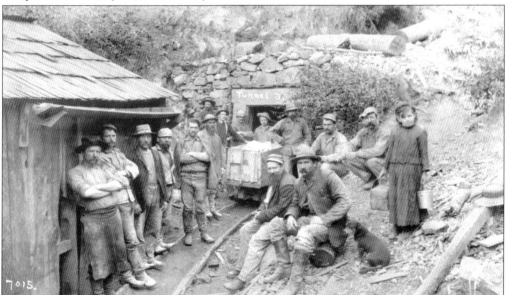

A group of haggard-looking miners, along with a young girl carrying lunch buckets, pose near the entrance to the hardrock Keystone Mine in Amador City in this c. 1890 image. Hardrock mining turned out to be more profitable than placer mining in Amador, like most of California, although as the name implies, it was considerably more difficult work that involved tunneling into rock in search of gold-bearing quartz veins. Most Amador mines produced relatively little gold compared to the amount of ore that was removed, although the ones that dug deepest generally produced the most. The Keystone was an exception; it produced over $24 million in gold during its lifetime despite being less than 3,000 feet deep. For a view inside this mine, see page 80. (Courtesy Amador County Archives.)

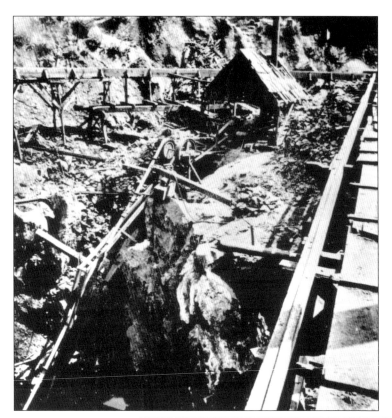

The reality of industrialized gold mining was somewhat less romantic than the lone-prospector ideal popularized in mining lore. As this photograph taken near Volcano c. 1866 illustrates, commercial placer-mining operations were quite complex and more than a little messy. Note the extensive arrangement of catwalks and shoring, arranged around a miner's shack at this site. (Courtesy Amador County Archives.)

Soldier's Gulch was a heavily mined area in Volcano and was just about mined out by the mid-1860s when this photograph was taken. That makes sense, as the gulch was the first place gold was discovered in town. This area is on the south side of town where Sutter Creek runs. (Courtesy Amador County Archives.)

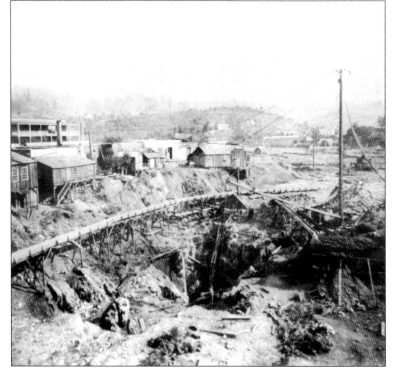

This 1866 image of placer miners shows the hard manual labor involved in this work. The crane-like object to the left was used to lift ore from the diggings into the dump box in the background, where workers would sift through it. Long after the mining years were over, tailing piles such as the one at the back became permanent fixtures of the landscape as small, unnatural-looking hills. Some have grown over with vegetation, but others (such as those visible along Highway 88 near the Jackson Valley Road junction at the old Newton copper mine) are still barren rock piles. (Courtesy Amador County Archives.)

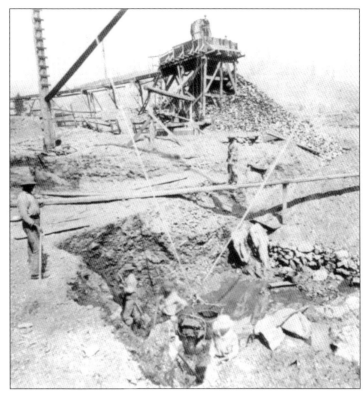

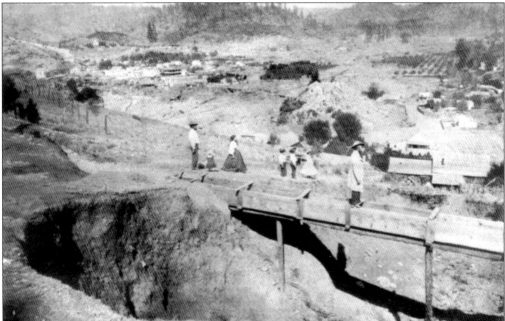

A family takes a walk near a mining flume in this 1860s–era image with a nice view of Volcano below them. The St. George Hotel can just barely be seen in the background at left of center, and the Masonic Roack is just above and to the left of the fellow walking in the flume. (Courtesy of Terry Grillo.)

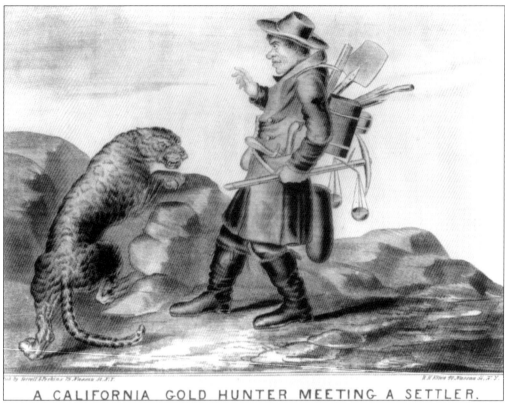

The popular image of the independent gold panner, or prospector, was of a well-equipped fellow like the one in this *c.* 1850 drawing, replete with shovels, picks, a scale, and of course knives to ward off mountain lions. The reality for many was much more industrialized than independent, with men working on crews in commercial mines. (Courtesy Amador County Archives.)

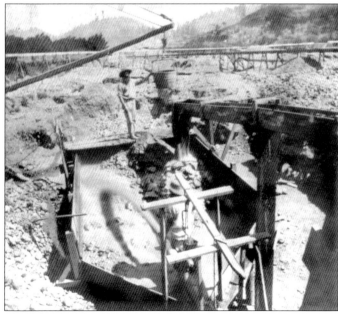

The miner in this *c.* 1866 image is working the dump box, where fresh-dug ore and dirt was dumped for sifting. (Courtesy Amador County Archives.)

The dump box required thorough cleaning from time to time given the large amounts of dirt and rock that could clog it. The expression of the gentleman at right indicates it was not among the more highly desired jobs of the gold fields. (Courtesy Amador County Archives.)

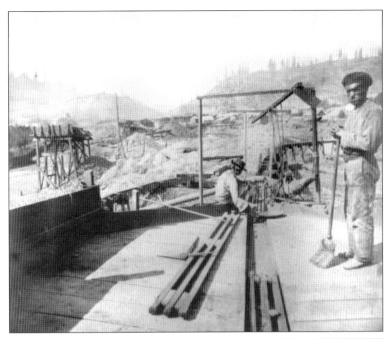

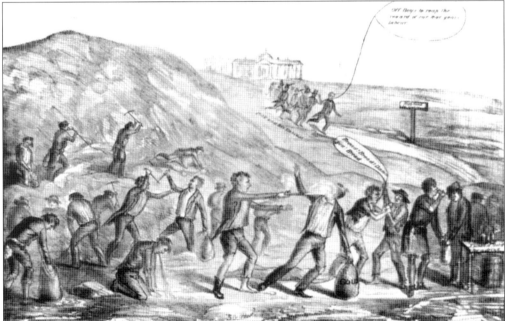

Hieronymous Bosch meets Currier and Ives in this grimly comic cartoon from around 1850. If the scenario here is to be believed, life in the gold fields had more in common with *Deadwood* than *Paint Your Wagon*. Much desperation occurs in the foreground, including a miner vomiting, another shooting a man in the face for his bag of gold, while various brawls and knife fights go on. One man accosts another for food, screaming, "Bread! Bread! Damn you! Bread!" In the background a group of politicians struts forward, with the leader saying, "Off boys to enjoy the fruits of our four years labor!" This is likely a dig at Pres. James K. Polk, as California was acquired from Mexico during his administration. (Courtesy Amador County Archives.)

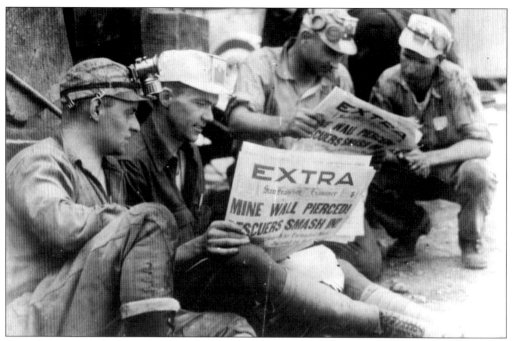

One of Amador's darkest chapters occurred on August 27, 1922, when a fire in the main shaft trapped 47 miners nearly 4,700 feet deep in the Argonaut Gold Mine in Jackson. Family, friends, coworkers, and people across the country waited for word of those trapped. Unfortunately it took three weeks for the rescuers to reach the men, and there were no survivors. Here miners catch up on the events of the tragedy. (Courtesy Amador County Archives.)

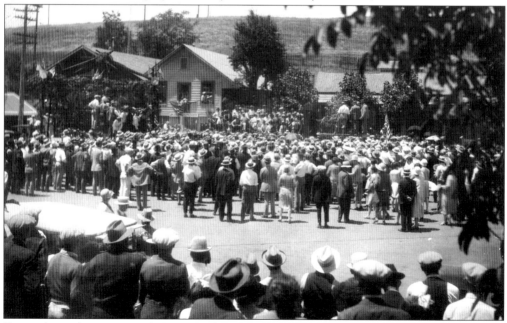

For weeks in the summer of 1922, people across the country were transfixed by the Argonaut disaster and eagerly sought updates as the situation grew more dire. Here a crowd of people waits for word of the miners' fates outside the mine. (Courtesy Amador County Archives.)

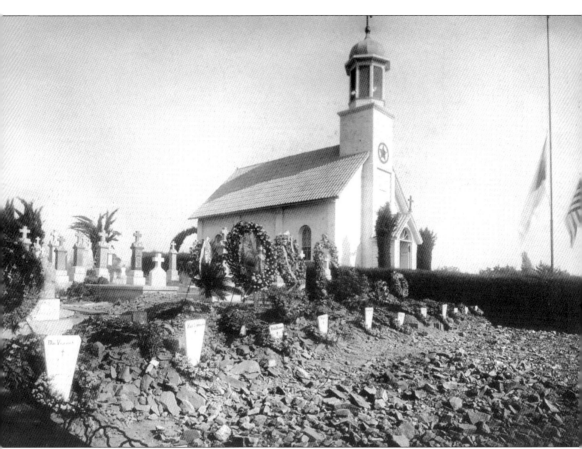

This was the heartbreaking outcome of the Argonaut disaster and the three-week rescue attempt—a series of graves at the Serbian Orthodox Church Cemetery in Jackson (not all the victims were buried here). The incident's staggering loss of 47 lives remains California's worst mining tragedy. The cause of the fire was not precisely known and was accorded to the overly broad term "incendiarism," a catchall term that could mean anything from poor wiring to intentional arson. Evidence at the site suggested the miners died from inhaling gases produced by the fire. The Argonaut's owners escaped punishment even though it was determined the mine had numerous safety violations. The mine continued to operate until 1942, producing over $25 million in gold during its lifetime, but its name is forever linked to this monumental tragedy. Many of the men who died were immigrants from Italy, Serbia, and Spain, and a good deal of them had no family in America. The 47 miners who perished were, in alphabetical order, Elmer Lee Bacheller, Peter Bagoye, Rafaelo Baldocchi, Rade Begoviche, D. Boleri, Eugene Buscaglia, John Caminada, Peter Cavaglieri, James Clayton, Paul DeLonga, Evan Ely, A. Fazzina, Edward William Fessell, V. Fidele, Charles T. Fitzgerald, Simone Francisconi, Battista Gamboni, Timothy E. Garcia, Maurice Gianetti, Giuseppe Giorza, Lucio Gonzales, Marko Janovich, Milos Jovanovich, Manuel Kosta, Jefto Kovac, Rade Lajovich, Antonio Leon, Luis Leon, Battista Manachino, Steve Marinovich, John Maslesa, Ernest Miller, Todore Miljanovich, Arthur William O'Berg, Charles O'Berg, Emanuel Olobardi, Pio Oliva, Aldino Piagneri, Elia Pavlovich, Giovanni Ruzzu, Domenico Simonde, Bert Seamans, Niko Stanicich, George L. Steinman, Daniele Villia, Mike Vujovich, and Cesare Zanardi. The Argonaut disaster is detailed in the 2004 book *47 Down: The 1922 Argonaut Gold Mine Disaster* by O. Henry Mace. (Courtesy Amador County Archives.)

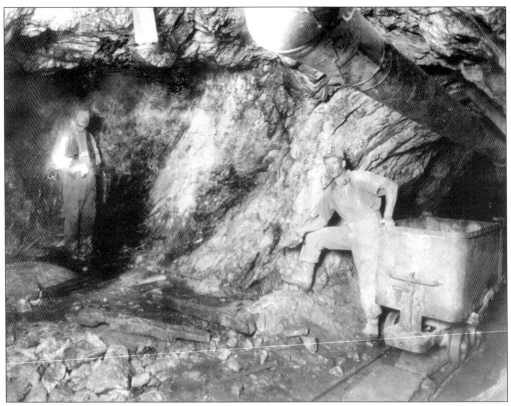

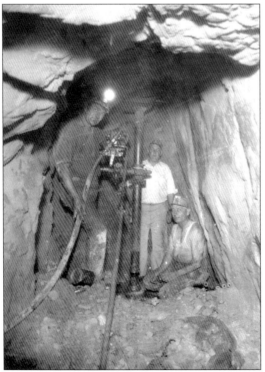

Hardrock mining is not for the claustrophobic, as this undated photograph from an unidentified Amador mine shows. Although this type of mining typically produced much higher yield than stream or surface (placer) mining, the scenery and surroundings were decidedly less pleasing. Amador is still pockmarked with many old mines such as this one; rusted tracks like these can occasionally be found heading into tunnels. Despite the novelty, such places are almost always unstable and unsafe to enter today. (Courtesy Amador County Archives.)

Hardrock miners in Amador normally made use of the most sophisticated equipment available, such as the hydraulic roof-jack device operated by these three men in the Lonesome Willow Tree Mine. (Courtesy Amador County Archives.)

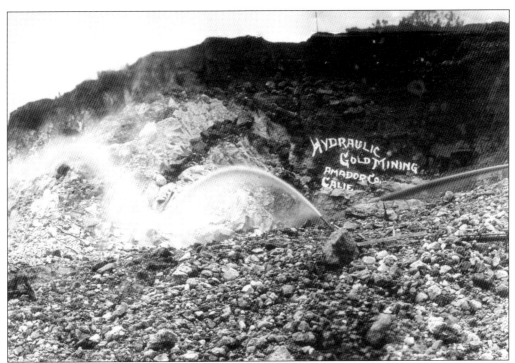

In this view of hydraulic mining at the Ludekins Mine, *c.* 1900, high-pressure monitors wash a hillside into rubble. (Courtesy Amador County Archives.)

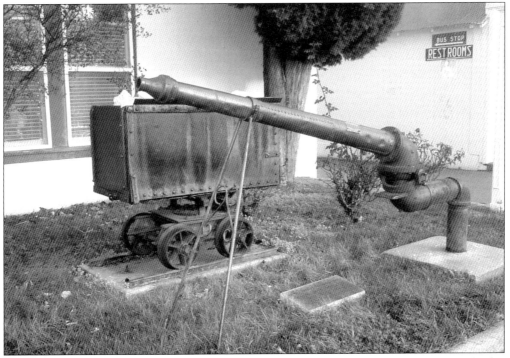

This is a present-day photograph of an old hydraulic monitor (alongside a mining cart) on display outside of the city hall in Sutter Creek. (Courtesy author.)

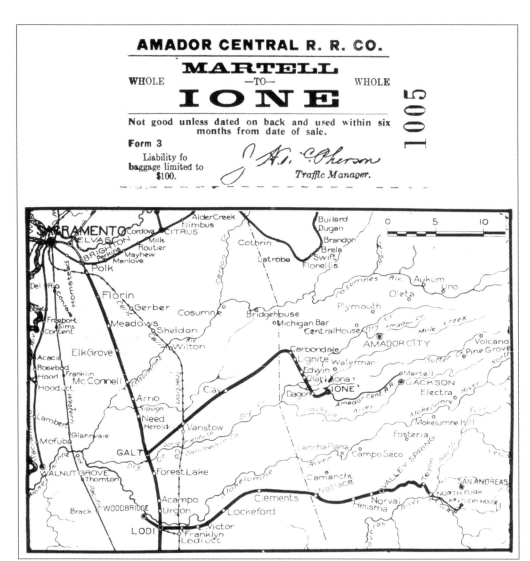

The Amador Central Railroad was in use (under various names and ownerships) from 1904 through 2004, running the 11.7 miles from Martell to Ione. It was the shortest standard-gauge rail line in regular use in the country. Ione was connected through the Amador Branch Railroad to Galt, some 27 miles away, and thus to the main rail lines between Sacramento and Stockton. It was incorporated in April 1904 as the Ione and Eastern Railroad before it was bought by Georgia Pacific and operated as Amador Central from 1909 through 1988. The last run of the Amador Central was in March 1997, though the line was reopened two years later and ran through 2004 under the ownership of Sierra Pacific Industries as the Amador Foothills Railroad. Many of the place names on the c. 1906 map above, which shows the line's connection to Galt, are no longer in use. (Courtesy Amador County Archives.)

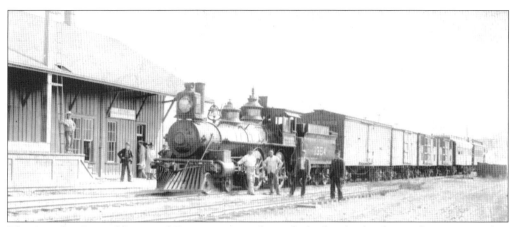

The Amador Central/Ione and Eastern was used mostly for freight, lumber and mining supplies specifically. Here the train pulls into the Ione station in this *c.* 1912 image, pulling a series of boxcars. (Courtesy Amador County Archives.)

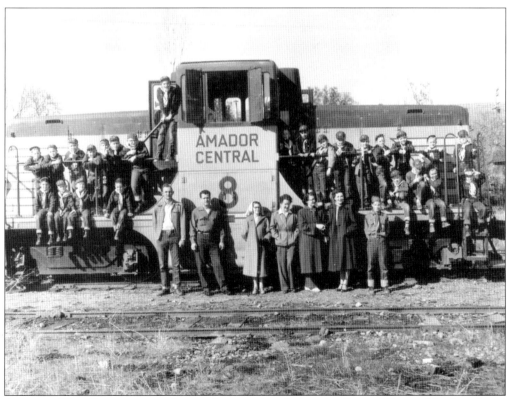

A group of Boy Scouts gets up close and personal with Amador Central Engine No. 8 in this *c.* 1962 photograph. (Courtesy Amador County Archives.)

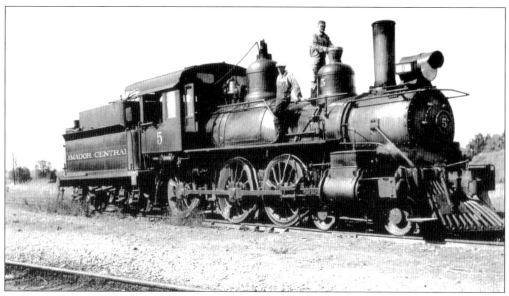

Two engineers pose atop the Amador Central's Engine No. 5 in this undated photograph. (Courtesy Amador County Archives.)

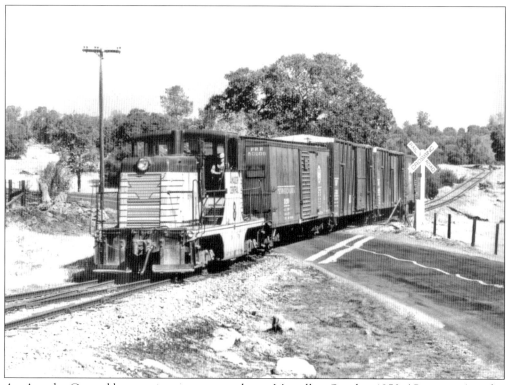

An Amador Central locomotive crosses a road near Martell in October 1950. (Courtesy Amador County Archives.)

Specialized equipment such as this log-loading forklift was needed by Amador Central to accommodate the heavy transportation needs of the lumber industry. (Courtesy Amador County Archives.)

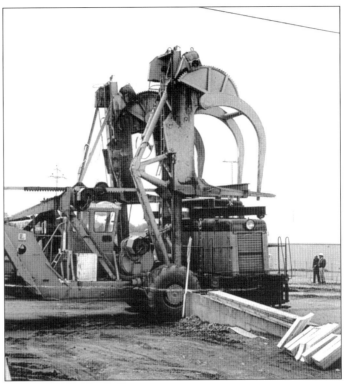

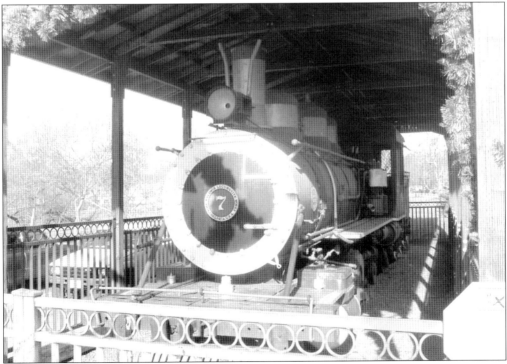

"Iron Ivan," also known as Amador Central Engine No. 7, can today be found on display in Ione Community Park. (Courtesy author.)

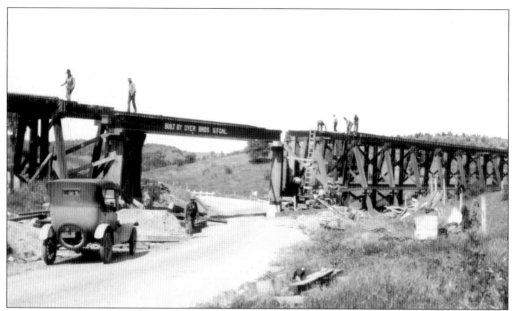

This *c.* 1939 image shows the Amador Central rail trestle under construction over what is now Highway 88 between Ione and Martell by the Dyer Brothers Iron Works of San Francisco. (Courtesy Amador County Archives.)

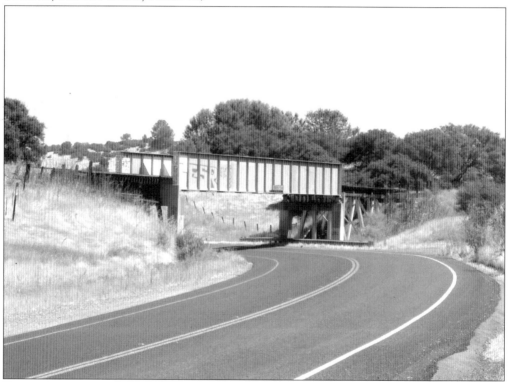

Here is the same view as above in 2006. The trestle is still there, looking none the worse for wear except for the graffiti. It was in use until Sierra Pacific Industries shut down the line in 2004. (Courtesy author.)

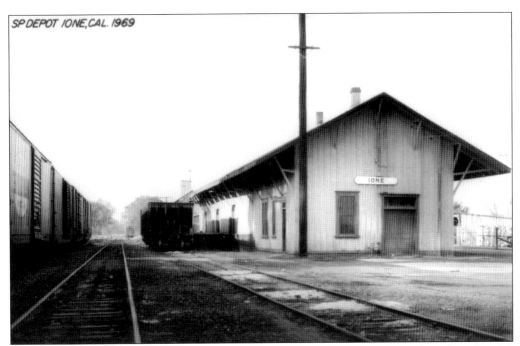

This postcard shows the Amador Central Ione station, identified here as the SP (Southern Pacific) Depot, in 1969. (Courtesy Amador County Archives.)

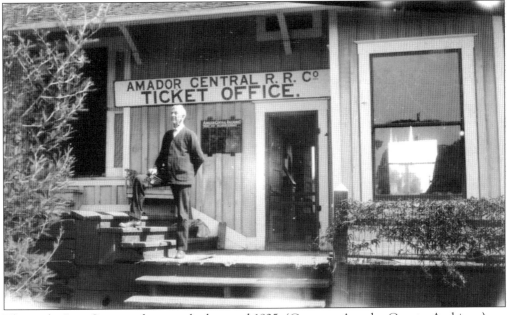

This is the Ione Station, photographed around 1925. (Courtesy Amador County Archives.)

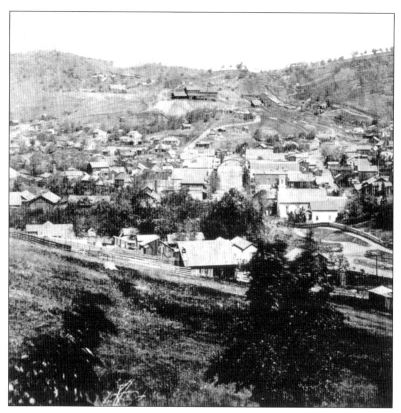

Sutter Creek, seen here *c.* 1875, became the most important supply center for local mines during the gold rush. Highway 49 passed directly through town for many years, but as of this writing, a bypass is in the works due to congestion in the downtown area. (Courtesy Amador County Archives.)

Ione was also a supply center, but its location closer to the valley also made it an agricultural center and rail hub. In 1876, it had about 600 residents, including roughly 100 Chinese who lived in the town's small Chinatown district. At that time, it had four churches, four general stores, one public school, and one brewery. Here is the town as it looked in 1866. (Courtesy Amador County Archives.)

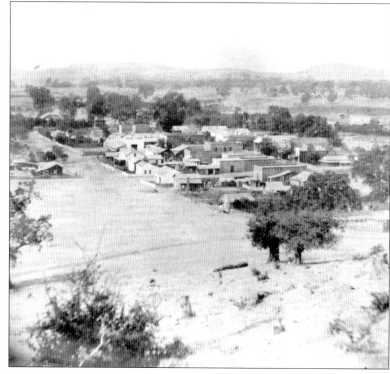

George Madeira, pictured here around 1865, built California's first amateur observatory in Volcano in 1860. He reported on a great number of findings, including sunspot activity and the "discovery" of the Great Comet of 1861—though that comet had already been discovered in Australia at the time. (News didn't travel as fast then as now.) He was also a mining engineer and geologist. A historic marker downtown now commemorates his observatory. (Courtesy Amador County Archives.)

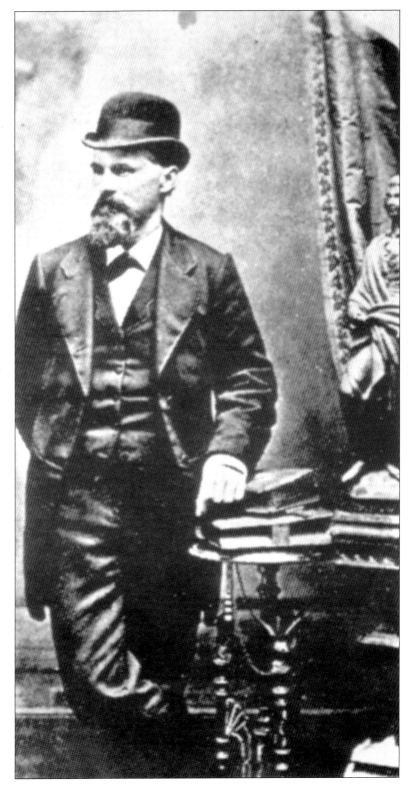

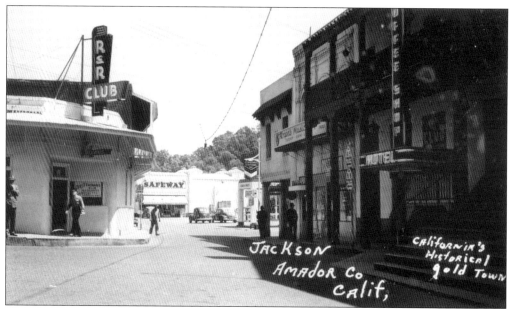

Here is a typical street scene in Jackson, c. 1945, at the intersection of Main and Water Streets. The R&R Club is now the Fargo Club, and the Safeway in the background has moved over to Martell. The building is currently used as a real estate office. (Courtesy Amador County Archives.)

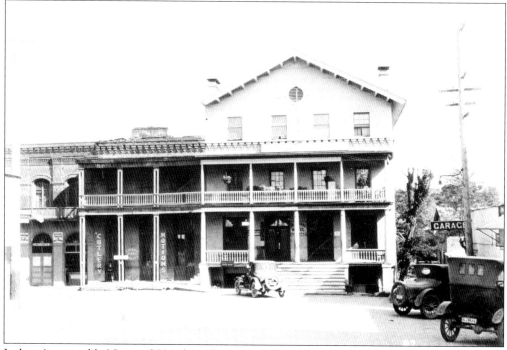

Jackson's venerable National Hotel, at the corner of Main and Water Streets, is still as popular a destination for gold country visitors as it was in this 1925 photograph. It was rebuilt at this location in 1863 at the site of an earlier hotel called the Louisiana. The hotel is built in the area where Jackson began—a natural spring where miners congregated in the late 1840s en route to various mines in the region. (Courtesy Amador County Archives.)

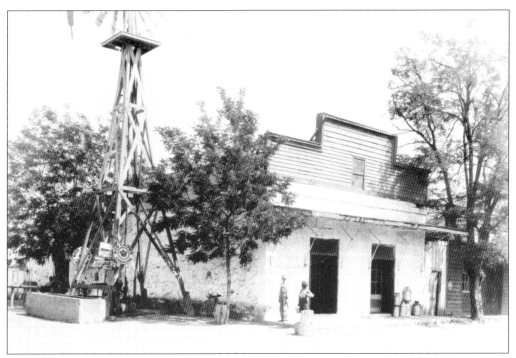

The Buena Vista Store, near Lake Camanche just south of Ione, was built in the 1850s in nearby Lancha Plana from stone blocks and moved to its present location in 1876. Then-owner John Fitzsimmons arranged for Chinese laborers to move the entire structure, piece by piece, to where it is now, supposedly because the ground at the original site held gold-bearing quartz. (Courtesy Amador County Archives.)

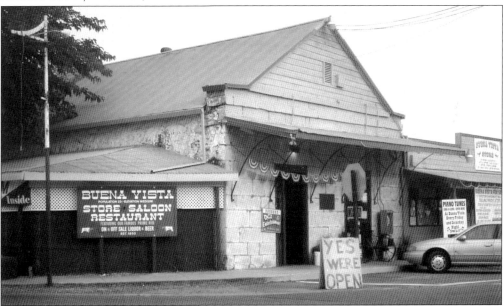

This is the Buena Vista Store in 2006. Much of the original masonry is still in use, still sturdy after more than 150 years. The roof timbers are made of Georgia pines "shipped 'round the Horn." The store is now a saloon and restaurant. Locals call it the BV. (Courtesy author.)

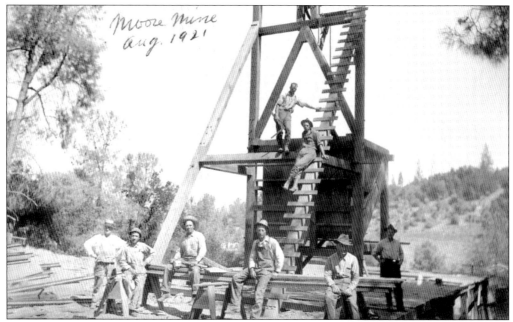

The Moore Mill, just south of Jackson, operated from the 1880s through 1929, though it was idle for some time during that period. Its shafts led to 2,300 feet, and ore was processed in a 20-stamp mill. (These are devices used to crush ore in search of gold; the stamps are heavy shafts used to break the ore and are driven by overhead camshafts.) During its lifetime, it produced about $564,000 of gold. These workers strike jaunty and defiant poses outside the mine in August 1921 as a new headframe is built. (Courtesy Amador County Archives.)

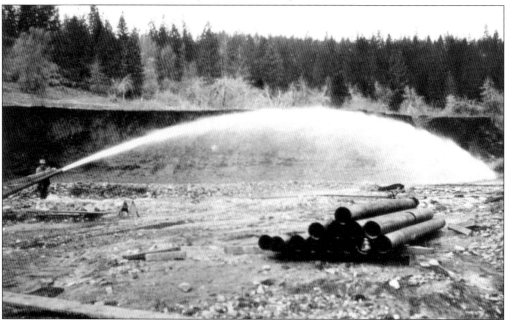

This is another view of the destructive force of hydraulic mining, captured at the Ludekins Mine in 1890 near present-day Aqueduct Road between Pine Grove and Pioneer. (Courtesy Amador County Archives.)

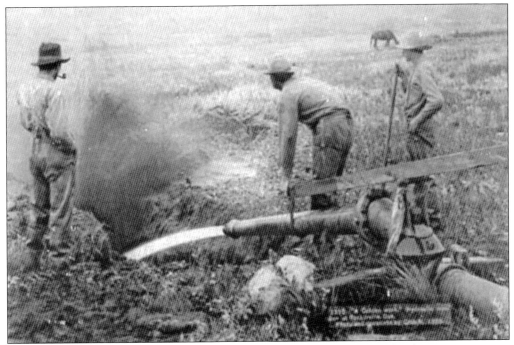

The workers in this 1890s–era image are aiming a water cannon, or hydraulic monitor, into a ditch in search of gold. It's entirely possible that the ditch wasn't there before they aimed the cannon at it. (Courtesy Amador County Archives.)

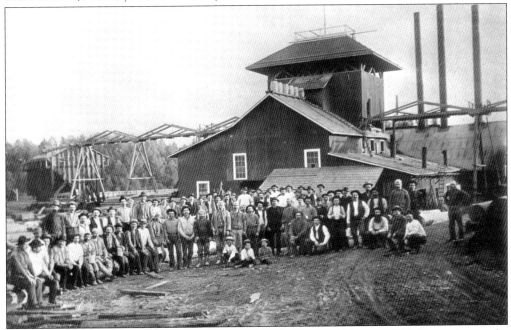

Employees of the Zeile Mine, just south of Jackson, are pictured here c. 1910. The mine used a large 16-stamp mill and produced over $5 million in gold. It operated from the 1860s through 1875, was idle for a time, and then reopened again in 1880. It continued operating through 1914. (Courtesy Amador County Archives.)

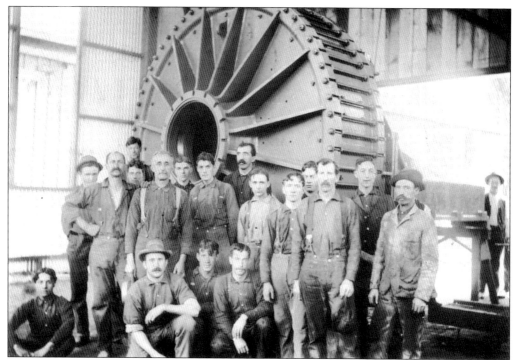

Knights Foundry, located on Eureka Street in Sutter Creek, is a California State Historic Landmark (one of 25 in Amador County). The foundry and machine shop was created in 1872 to make heavy equipment for the mining and lumber industries in Amador and other foothills areas. It is the last surviving specimen of a shop run by water power—the same system of water diverted from creeks into turbines that is used by hydroelectric power plants, but in this case, it was used to power various machinery. (Courtesy Amador County Archives.)

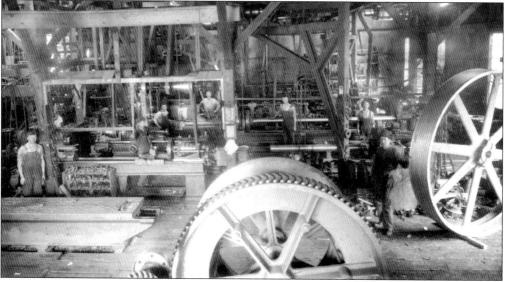

Workers at Knights Foundry stand amidst the humming water-powered machinery in the extensive shop. The foundry can be seen, and occasionally toured, today. (Courtesy Amador County Archives.)

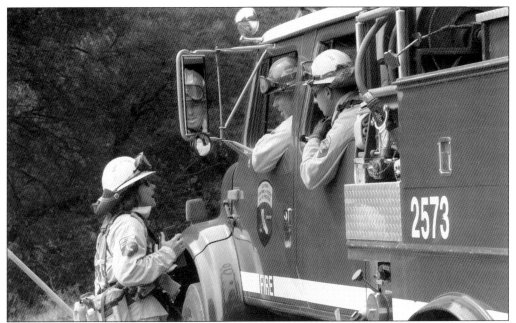

Amador's wooded countryside makes the county especially susceptible to fire danger, whether in the brushy lowlands or the forested upcountry region. On September 28, 2004, a large fire sparked by arcing PG&E power lines in the Tiger Creek area came fairly close to houses in the Sierra Highlands area. In this image by celebrated contemporary Amador photographer Bill Lavallie, firefighters confer as the blaze burns in the steep area just off Tiger Creek and Black Prince Roads. The fire was put out quickly thanks to the fast response of regional and state fire crews, but it underscored the dangers of living in Amador, where all of the major towns have had disastrous fires at one time or another. (Courtesy Bill Lavallie.)

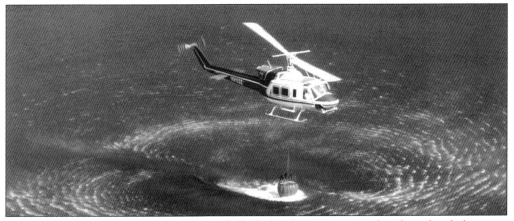

The 2004 Tiger Creek fire was put out with the help of air support, with at least four helicopters and two planes helping in the fight. In this image, a helicopter dips a water bucket into the Tiger Creek afterbay just west of the Tiger Creek Powerhouse before dumping water on the fire in the nearby hills. This fire ended in just a day, but two weeks later, another blaze in the Salt Springs/ Bear River area about 15 miles north of Pioneer burned for several days, charring 17,000 acres and forcing the evacuation of the Bear River Reservoir resort area. More than 800 firefighters, some from as far away as Arizona, battled the blaze from a command center at Highway 88 and Ellis Road. It was denoted the "Power Fire." (Courtesy Bill Lavallie.)

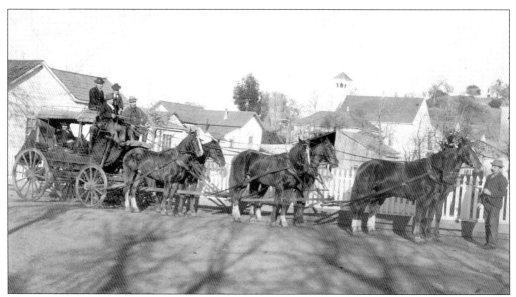

A stagecoach and horse team gears up in Ione for parts beyond Amador. Supposedly, after this 1899 photograph was taken, this stage was later held up by bandits during its journey at an area called Cyclone Station.

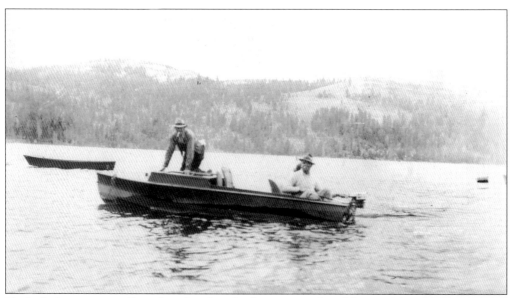

Caples Lake was originally in Amador, though it's now part of neighboring Alpine County. In this c. 1940 image, Warren Taylor (right) and A. Johnson ply the scenic lake's surface quite close to the famed Kirkwood resort. Taylor, grandson of original Kirkwood resort owner Zack Kirkwood, sold the Kirkwood property to ski developers after the original resort closed in 1966. The developers later opened Kirkwood Mountain Resort in 1972. (Courtesy Amador County Archives.)

Pictured here is still more fun on the Fourth of July, Amador style. On Plymouth's Main Street in 1903, this ornately dressed group of girls, wearing sashes denoting various states of the union, rides by the Harvey House where a sign reads "Meals at all hours." (Courtesy Amador County Archives.)

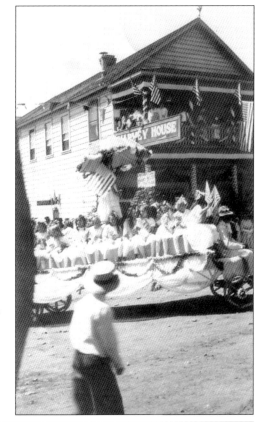

This is Fourth of July fun in Amador 88 years later, and it shows no sign of abating. In 2006, a group of residents in the Amador Pines section of Pioneer gussied up their tractors (normally reserved for such mundane roles as clearing brush and snow) with flags, bunting, and general-purpose joie de vivre for a parade through the upcountry region. (Courtesy Greg Bortolin.)

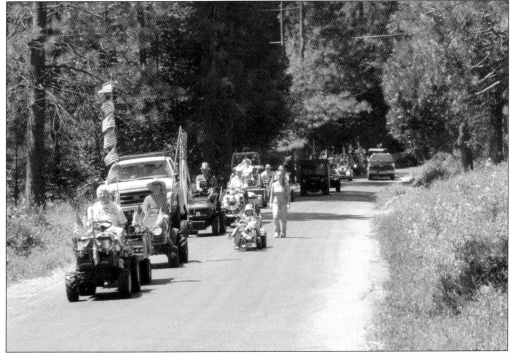

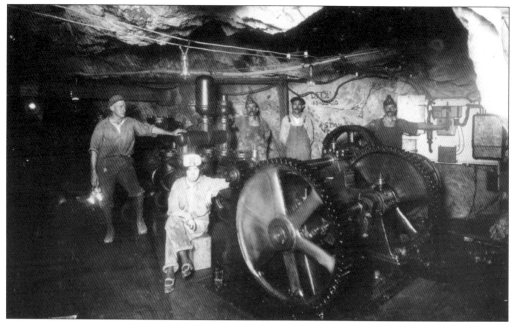

The Keystone Mine in Amador City, formed from several claims originating in 1851, became one of the Mother Lode's most profitable mines. It made more than $24 million in its lifetime (from the 1850s through 1919 and then from 1933 to 1942), and shareholders at one point had dividends of over $500 per share. Pictured here around 1905 is a group of workers in the depth of the mine, as superintendent B. I. Hoxsie stands to the left holding carbide lights. (Courtesy Amador County Archives.)

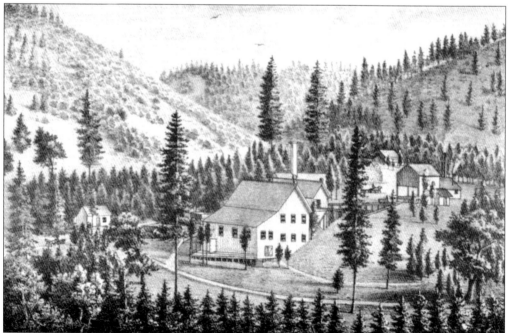

This c. 1880 drawing depicts the workings of the Hanford and Downs mine in Volcano. See page 41 for a photograph of this company's offices on Main Street. (Courtesy Amador County Archives.)

Three

POWER TO THE PEOPLE!

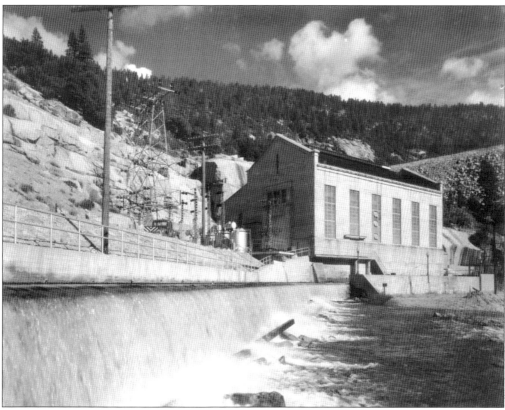

Pacific Gas and Electric Company (PG&E) has a substantial presence in Amador through its ambitious Mokelumne River Project, an elaborate power-generation development that involves vast areas in both Alpine and Amador Counties. Starting at Blue Lakes in Alpine, the company early in the 20th century set up an elaborate series of channels, diversion dams, reservoirs, flumes, penstocks, and power plants that today provides over one million kilowatt hours per year—enough to power about 200,000 homes (air conditioners and video-game consoles included). The project provides relatively "clean" energy through water-powered turbine plants, but it is not without controversy. In recent years, there have been efforts to restore water flows in the Mokelumne and its tributaries that had been diverted to the power plants, and environmental organizations, such as the Foothill Conservancy in Pioneer, constantly seek balance with PG&E's work in these mountains. Pictured here in 1957 is the Salt Springs power plant, the uppermost of PG&E's hydro-generation facilities. Also in Amador are the Tiger Creek and Electra powerhouses, in Pioneer and Jackson respectively. (Courtesy PG&E.)

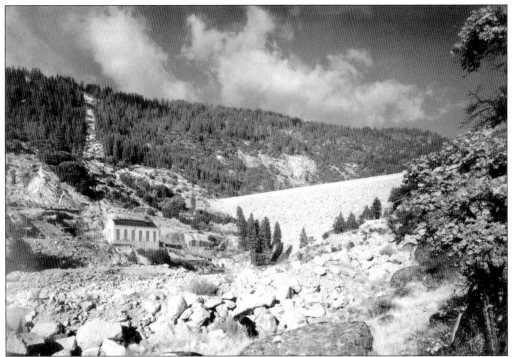

The massive scale of the Salt Springs Dam can be seen against the powerhouse in this 1957 image of the Salt Springs power plant on the Mokelumne River. (Courtesy PG&E.)

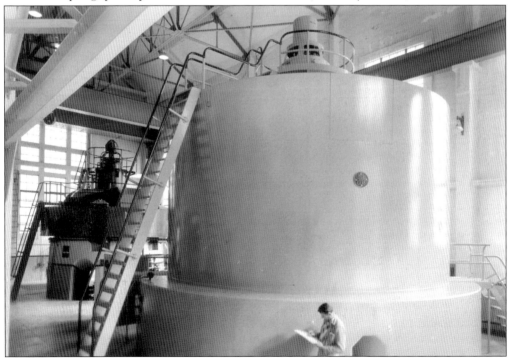

This 1957 photograph of the interior of the Salt Springs powerhouse shows the size of the generators contained within. This powerhouse generates about 32 megawatts. (Courtesy PG&E.)

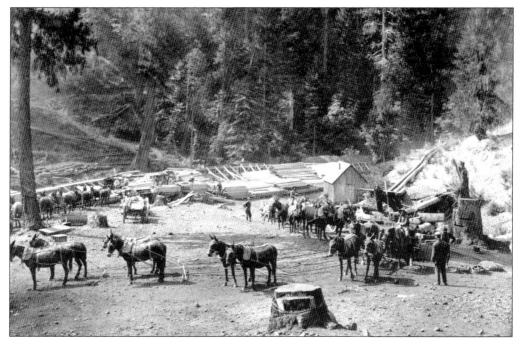

Construction of the powerhouses along the Mokelumne was a massive undertaking and one that started during a time without much in the way of automation. "Primitive" methods, such as this horse-drawn lumber wagon, were used to complete the task. The Tiger Creek Sawmill was located above Tiger Creek and is pictured here around 1910 with workers processing lumber for power plants. (Courtesy PG&E.)

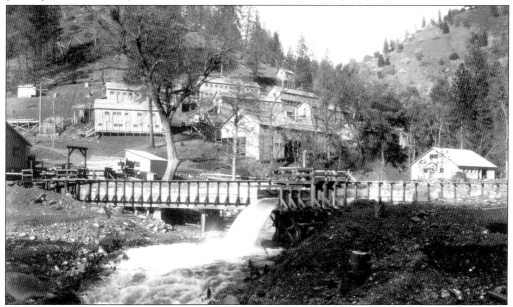

This is the Tiger Creek complex in 1930 just before the opening of the powerhouse the following year. The place doesn't look like this anymore, but there are still a good number of buildings—some employee housing and some for the conference center—clinging to the hillsides above the powerhouse. (Courtesy PG&E.)

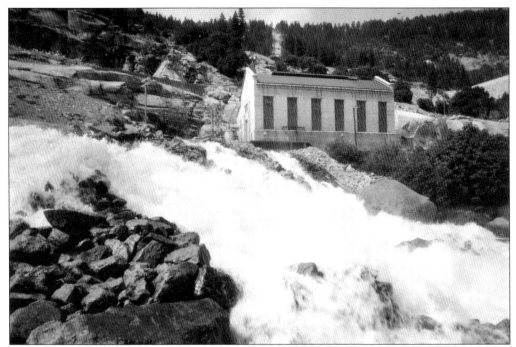

The Salt Springs powerhouse is in the Eldorado National Forest at about 4,000 feet above sea level. It gets power from water in the adjacent Salt Springs Reservoir that travels about 440 feet through a tube (or penstock, in power plant terms) into the turbine generators. The terrain around the powerhouse is quite rough, as this 1954 photograph shows. (Courtesy PG&E.)

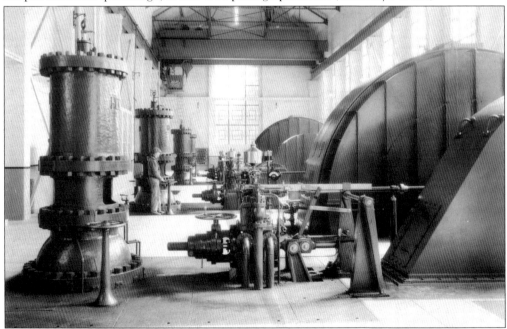

This photograph from 1931 shows the interior of the Tiger Creek powerhouse in Pioneer and the metallic outer casings of the turbine wheels. The water pressure is immense within these devices so the coverings were made very strong indeed. (Courtesy PG&E.)

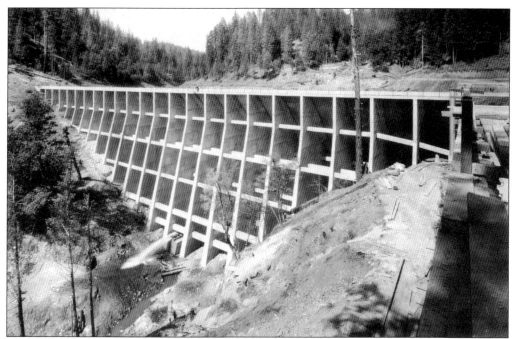

This imposing structure, above, is the dam for the Tiger Creek Regulatory Reservoir, a small man-made lake that is fed from diversion channels and flumes at higher elevations. The water fills up this lake, and from the dam, a series of gates lets the water into the penultimate flume before the powerhouse itself. Below is the picturesque surface of the lake as seen from above the dam. These images are from 1931, just after the dam's completion, though it looks almost exactly the same today. (Courtesy PG&E.)

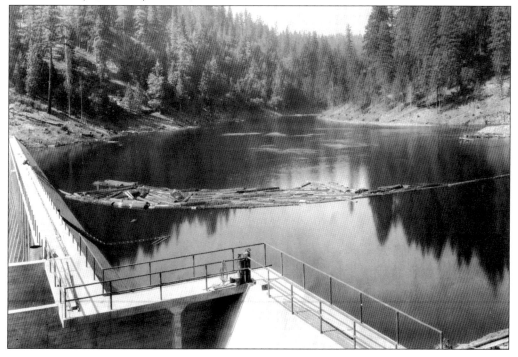

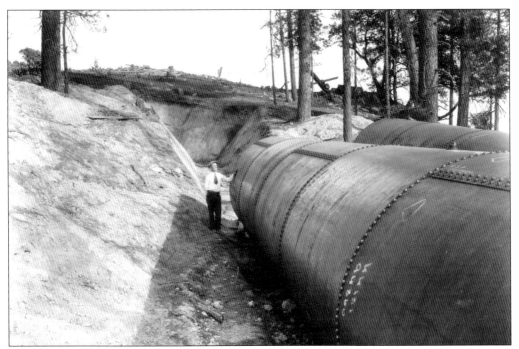

The Tiger Creek powerhouse uses a massive penstock, about eight feet in diameter, to drop the water downhill into the turbines. In this 1930 image, a worker inspects the pipe prior to the plant's opening. Note the massive cuts into the hillside. (Courtesy PG&E.)

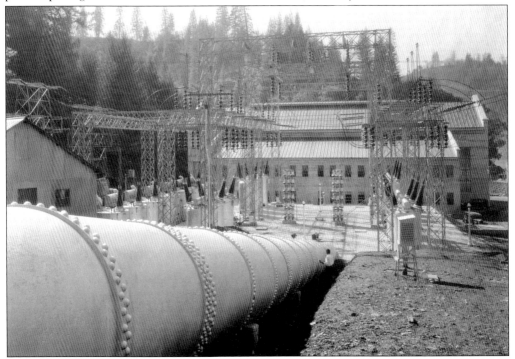

The penstock, shown here in 1931 leading into the Tiger Creek plant, drops water 1,200 feet down from a small collecting reservoir (or forebay) into the turbines. (Courtesy PG&E.)

This 1931 image shows the interior of one of the wheels that drive the turbines at Tiger Creek. Note that the nozzle is just inches away from the wheel; the deep, low groan produced by this mechanism can be heard for about a mile. The parking lot at the powerhouse has a complete wheel like this one on display. (Courtesy PG&E.)

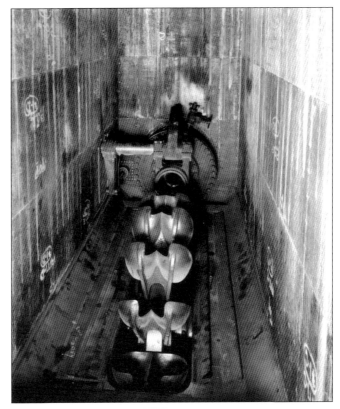

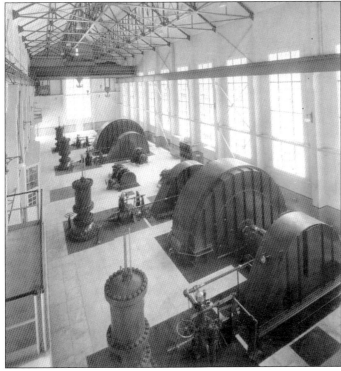

Here is an overhead view of the main turbine room at Tiger Creek, taken in 1931 just after the plant opened. These turbines provide 58 megawatts of power—enough to supply about 55,000 homes. (Courtesy PG&E.)

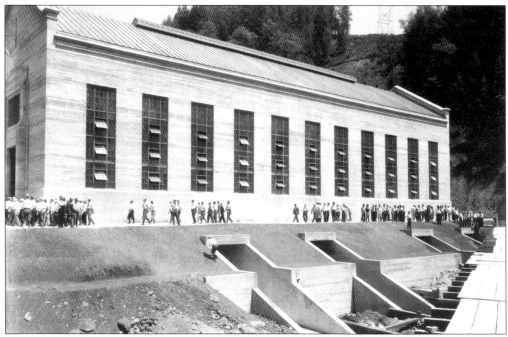

At Tiger Creek's 1931 opening, a large crowd of PG&E workers, some in short pants, take a victory lap of sorts around the main structure. The facility today also houses a conference center and quite a bit of employee housing in addition to a maintenance yard and administrative offices. (Courtesy PG&E.)

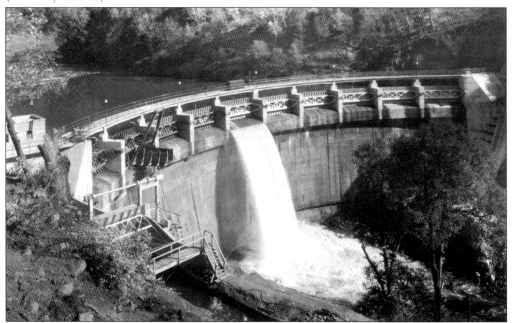

This is the dam at the western end of the Tiger Creek afterbay, where water collects and merges back with the Mokelumne River's main flow after having gone through the powerhouse. From this dam, the river returns to normal for a while, though further diversions occur downstream to feed the Electra powerhouse in Jackson and the West Point plant in Calaveras County. (Courtesy PG&E.)

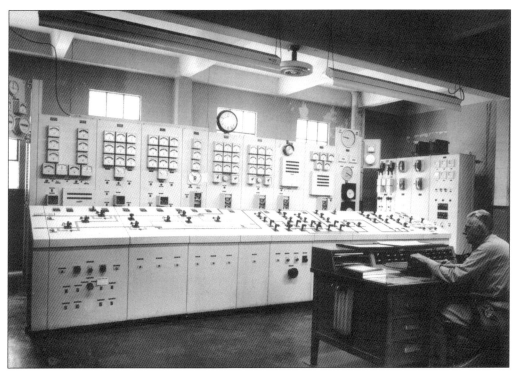

Pictured here is the main control console for Tiger Creek's power output shortly after the plant's completion in 1931. The gentleman at the control desk at right could probably cause some real havoc if he was in a bad mood. (Courtesy PG&E.)

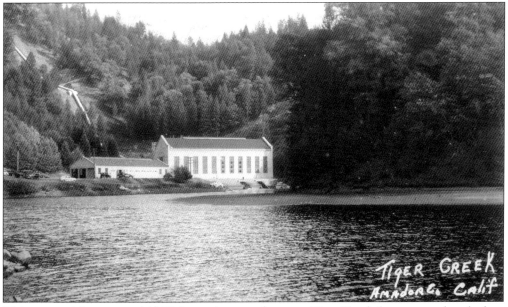

This postcard from around 1946 shows the powerhouse at Tiger Creek from across the afterbay, along with a garage structure at left and the penstock going up the hill behind it. The garage, now remodeled, houses maintenance and offices, and a large conference center building has been added to its left. (Courtesy PG&E.)

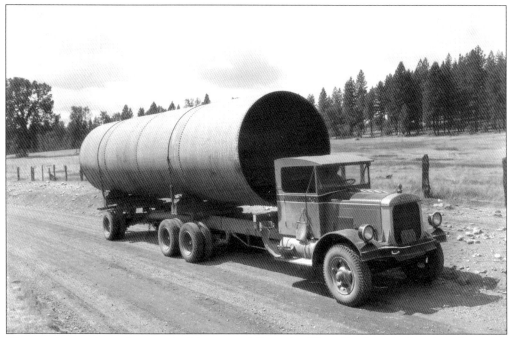

The massive sections of penstock piping were delivered to Tiger Creek and other Amador power plants by heavy equipment like this truck. This image is from 1930. (Courtesy PG&E.)

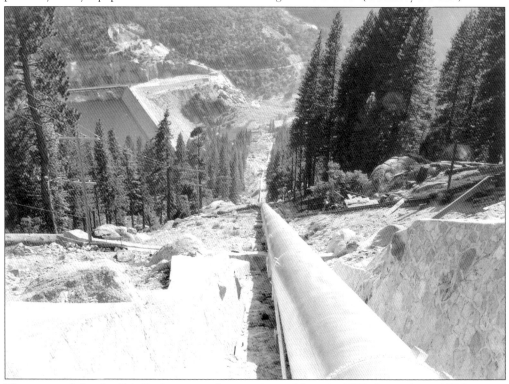

The penstock for the Salt Springs powerhouse, pictured here in 1957, drops about 400 feet into the turbines. (Courtesy PG&E.)

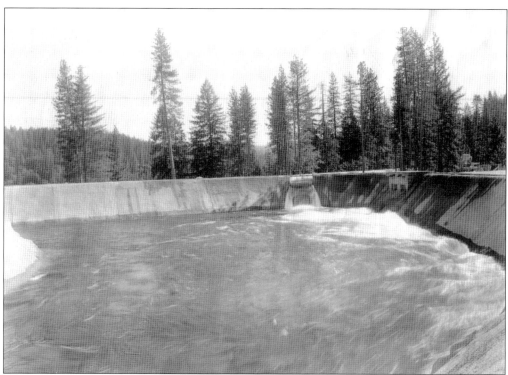

In this 1931 photograph is the Tiger Creek forebay, a small reservoir where water collects just before dropping through the penstock into the plant. This concrete-lined pool is fenced off, but locals still manage to fish here by throwing a line over the fence. Decent fishing is rumored. (Courtesy PG&E.)

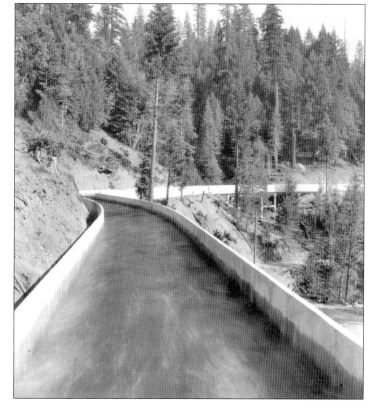

Here is a 1931 image of the Tiger Creek canal, a diversion channel that carries water from the Mokelumne River into the regulatory reservoir for use in the power plant. After the water goes through the plant, it is "reunited" with the Mokelumne River flow. (Courtesy PG&E.)

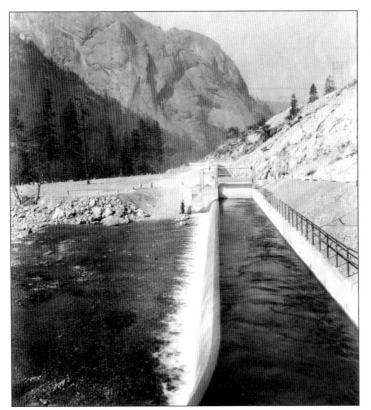

The Tiger Creek canal wends its way through diverse mountain scenery from the Salt Springs area all the way to Pioneer. Unfortunately innertubing is impractical in the canal due to low overcrossings like this one. (Courtesy PG&E.)

Mother Nature plays some interesting tricks with water at the Salt Springs Reservoir. This 1967 image depicts a "spill" some distance from the dam (the top of which can be seen at left behind the tree). These events occasionally happen during times of heavy snow runoff and just occurred again in 2006. The 1967 spill had water volumes as high as 3,250 cubic feet per second. (Courtesy PG&E.)

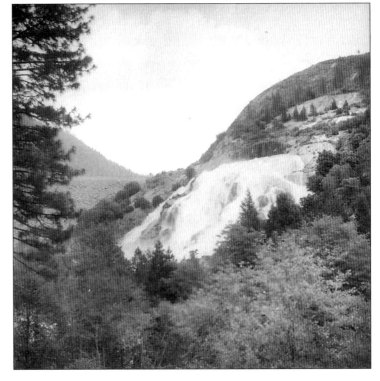

Four

Goin' Up the Country

Amador's upcountry region has world-class wilderness and scenery, similar to what one finds in the Tahoe and Yosemite regions, yet remains relatively uncrowded. This 1965 image of canoeists on Silver Lake on Highway 88, about 40 miles east of Pioneer and just before Kirkwood Ski Resort, looks remarkably similar to today's lake views—pristine, boulder-strewn expanses studded with alpine trees and shrubs. Silver Lake, among a handful of beautiful lakes in the upcountry area near the border of Alpine County, is a perennial favorite for fishing, hiking, and swimming. Large swaths of protected wilderness, including the El Dorado National Forest and the Mokelumne Wilderness, are in the Amador/Alpine region. (Courtesy Amador County Archives.)

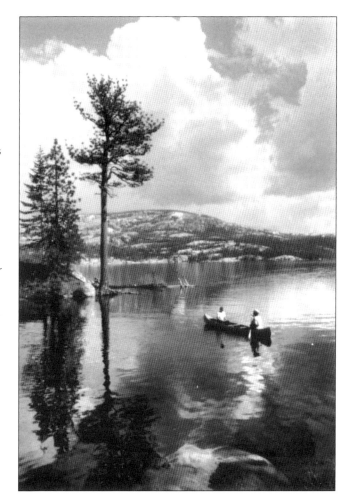

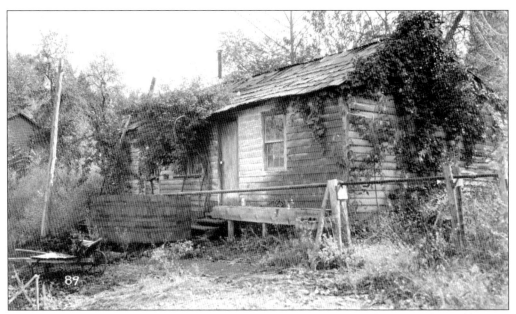

When one travels east on Highway 88 from Jackson, Pine Grove is where Amador really starts to "get country." It was always thus, as this 1930s-era image of what is purported to be the first house built in Pine Grove shows. This house, in ruins, is on Highway 88, about two miles west of todays Pine Grove. Pine Grove was known as a temperance center, which is in contrast to the hard-drinking towns all around it. (Courtesy Amador County Archives.)

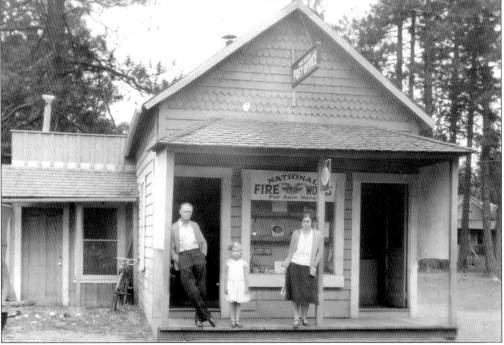

Today's modern post offices may have "all mod cons," but they're hard-pressed to match the charm of the old-world post offices. This is Pine Grove's around 1920, and the folks on the porch are most likely postmaster Anna Dennison and family. (Courtesy Amador County Archives.)

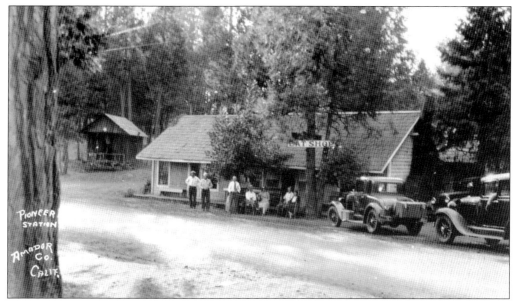

Pioneer Station was built in the 1920s, although its log construction makes it seem older. The Barnhart family owned the place when this photograph was taken *c.* 1925. The twin-tree formation at the right still exists today. (Courtesy author.)

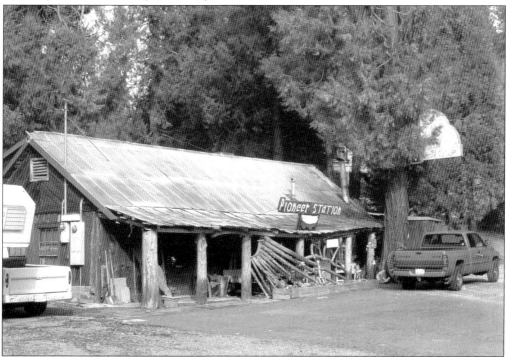

Pioneer Station, seen here in 2005, is today used as a private residence. For many years, however, it was a community store and social center. Its location at Defender Grade and Highway 88 made it a convenient stop for miners, lumbermen, and ranchers in the area, as Defender Grade was for many years the only route south to the West Point Bridge and into Calaveras County (at least until Red Corral Road was built). (Courtesy Amador County Archives.)

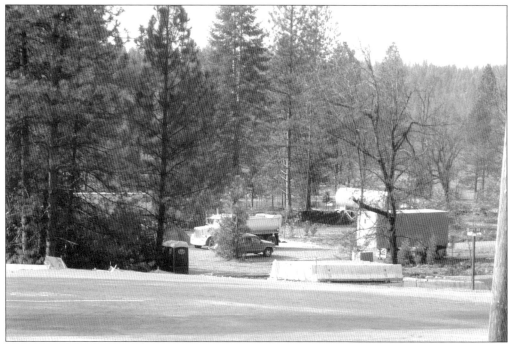

Construction sites like this are now fairly common in the area around Mace Meadows and Sierra Highlands. The word is out about the upcountry lifestyle and developers are moving in, although the scale of the projects is usually fairly small due to lot size and water requirements. This 2005 image is from the intersection of Silver Drive and Highway 88 in the Barton/Buckhorn area. (Courtesy author.)

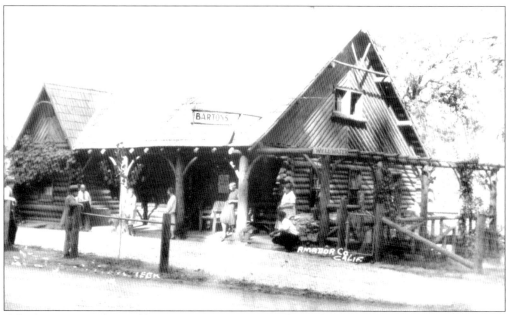

A little ways past the Buckhorn area, near Tiger Creek Road and Highway 88, was the original Barton roadhouse for which the area just past Silver Drive is named. It is pictured here around 1915. (Courtesy Amador County Archives.)

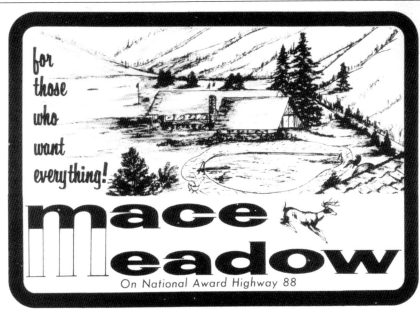

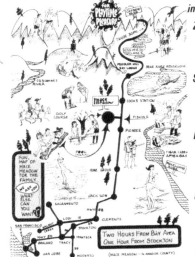
The Mace Meadows development, near Highway 88 and Silver Drive, has been a very successful one thanks in no small part to a well-maintained golf course and amenities for year-round living. This ad from 1966 touts the "imperishable investment" of a Mace Meadows domicile (and it's hard to dispel the logic, as houses that cost under $10,000 in the mid-1960s now fetch upwards of $300,000), the "sparkling mountain air," and the prospect of "just plain loafing" among many possible activities. Renting one's house out during the ski season promised an income of up to $75 per week. The ad's ominous ending note, suggesting that "never again can more be offered at today's prices and terms," makes one feel sad for the hundreds of millions who missed out. (Courtesy Greg Bortolin.)

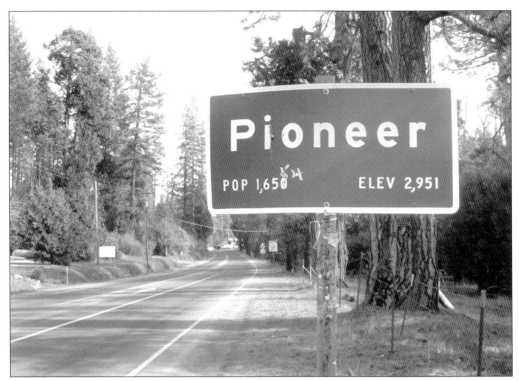

The population of Pioneer is slowly growing as more people discover the unique charms of upcountry living. (Courtesy author.)

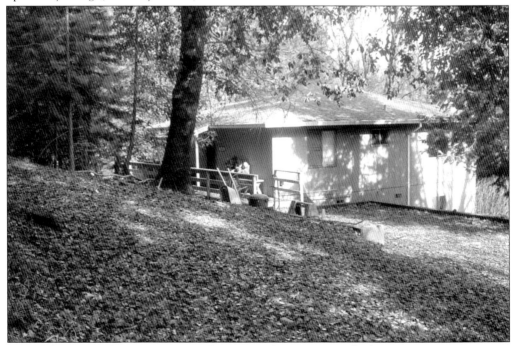

The subdivisions radiating out from Highway 88 in the Pioneer area harbor many quaint 1960s–era cabins like this one in Sierra Highlands. (Courtesy author.)

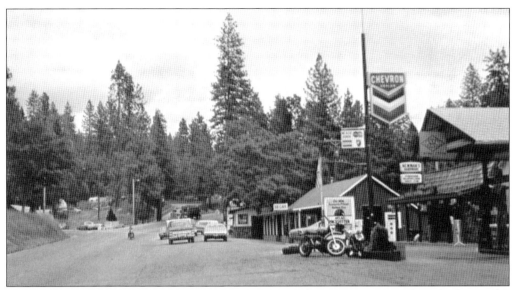

The "main drag" of Pioneer is pictured here in 1975. The town grew significantly during the construction of the Tiger Creek powerhouse and dam, but unlike other boomtowns around large-scale projects, it continued to grow modestly through the years. This postcard (the only known postcard of Pioneer) says there was once "wide-open gambling" in Café 88, pictured here at center. That building now houses a thrift shop and, for a while, a sorely missed head shop. The building in the foreground was the original location of Newman's Hardware. (Courtesy Amador County Archives.)

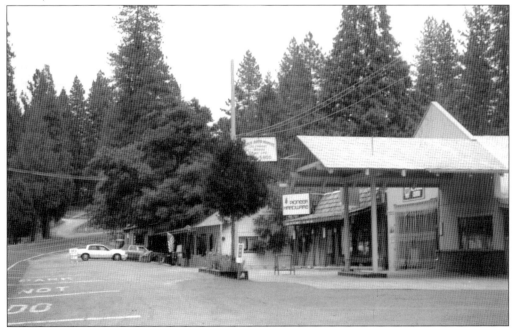

This is the same view as above seen in 2006. The original Newman's Hardware had been replaced by Pioneer Ace Hardware and moved uphill near Buckhorn to Newman Center on Tiger Creek Road. Newman's was a Pioneer institution for many years. It operated until 2006 when it was purchased and replaced by Warren and Sons Hardware at the same site. (Courtesy author.)

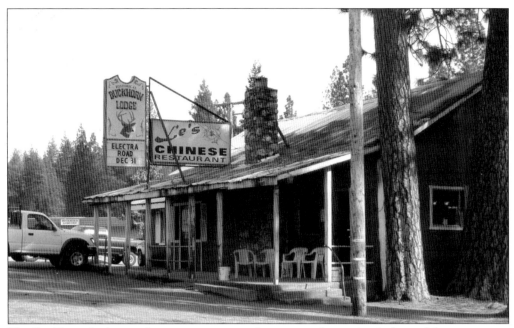

The Buckhorn Lodge is a longtime upcountry hangout and watering hole, and for many years the building held the esteemed Le's Chinese Restaurant, which moved closer to Defender Grade in 2006. The lodge (and very likely some sort of predecessor from the mining days) has seen much use through the years, as Tiger Creek Road was improved early on to gain access to the Mokelumne River's water for miners and settlers alike. (Courtesy author.)

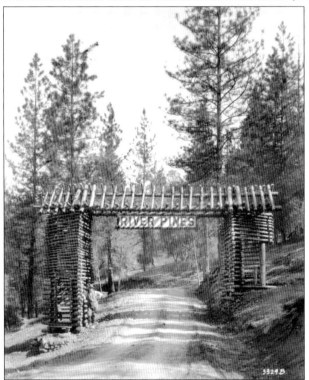

River Pines was originally developed by Roy and Helen Brooke in 1927 as a place where middle-class people could buy a vacation cabin. They found a suitable spot along the Cosumnes River, and the rest is history. (Courtesy Amador County Archives.)

Tragedy Springs is named for a tragic attack on three scouts, supposedly by Native Americans, in June 1848. A blaze was carved into this fir tree to commemorate the killing at the time. It reads, "To the memory of Daniel Browell, Ezrah H. Allen, and Henderson Cox who was supposed to have been murdered and buried by Indians on the night of the 27th of June 1848." The original blaze was removed from the fir tree at Tragedy Springs and moved to the Gold Discovery Museum in Coloma. (Courtesy Amador County Archives.)

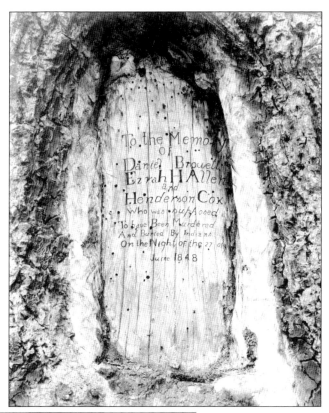

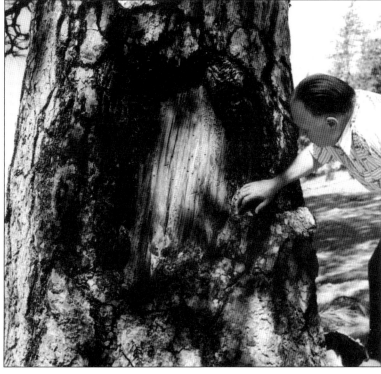

This 1970s–era image shows a lumber official inspecting a blaze on a tree used as a marker by the forty-niners along Old Emigrant Road. (Photograph by Larry Cenotto; courtesy Amador County Archives.)

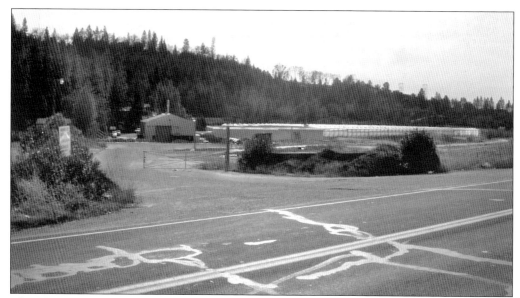

The old cedar mill sat on this spot in Pioneer for many years, near Buckhorn Plaza. Among other things, it milled cedar blocks that were used to manufacture pencils, and two gigantic pencils guarded the gates to the mill. The site, pictured here in 2005, is now used as an organic tomato farm (those are greenhouses in the image), but the giant pencils survived, as seen below. (Courtesy author.)

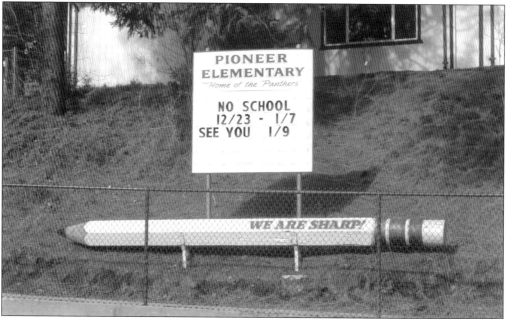

One of the cedar mill's giant guardian pencils, which once sat proudly upright at the mill's entrance, sits today on its side at Pioneer Elementary School, just across the highway from the old mill site. The slogan "We are Sharp!" is undoubtedly an allusion to the quaint, now-forgotten art of sharpening one's pencil, but in this case it is applied in a clever manner to imply that the school's pupils boast an unusually high level of perception and intelligence. The other giant pencil is at the Amador Museum in Jackson. This photograph is from 2005. (Courtesy author.)

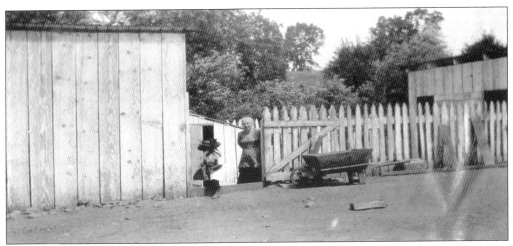

Fiddletown is a quaint little town in the northern part of Amador. It was called Oleta for a time before it was changed back to Fiddletown. It was also the setting for Western author Bret Harte's story "An Episode of Fiddletown" and was one of Mark Twain's gold country getaways. Here is a street scene in town around 1910. (Courtesy Amador County Archives.)

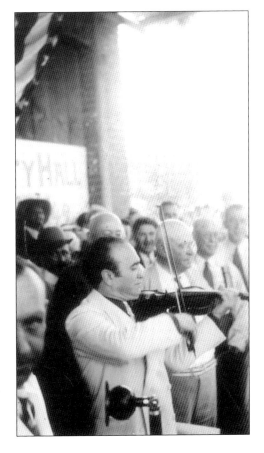

Renowned violinist David Rubinoff came to Fiddletown in 1934 to help celebrate the arrival of electricity to the town. The pate of the man directly behind Rubinoff belongs to county supervisor Ostrom. Today the Fiddletown Fiddlers Jam usually takes place every September. The origin of the name Fiddletown is a topic of some dispute, though it is said that the original settlers here mined during wet weather and fiddled outside in dry spells. There is also a rumor that the older miners were annoyed by the younger men's habit of "fiddling around." (Courtesy Amador County Archives.)

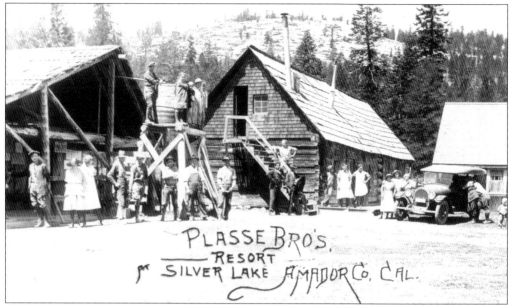

Plasse's Resort is situated near Silver Lake along the original emigrant trail blazed by the Mormon Battalion as a route to Salt Lake City. It is recognized as one of California's oldest campgrounds, having been founded in 1853 by Frenchman Ramón Pierre Plasse. The resort has long been a favorite upcountry destination and today hosts lots of RVs, campers, and boaters alike. Here the staff poses for a photograph in this 1930 postcard. (Courtesy Amador County Archives.)

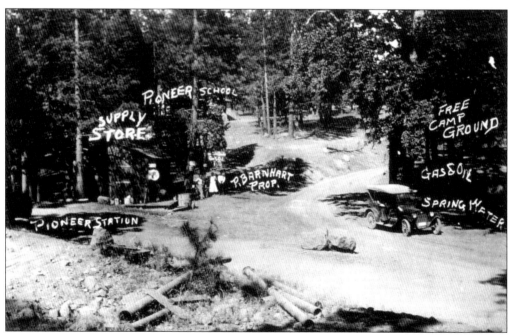

Pioneer started out as a supply station for upcountry types and PG&E workers, though it has evolved into a nebulous realm of cozy subdivisions in the pines since then. Here is the Pioneer Station area c. 1925, near the intersection of Highway 88 and Defender Grade. Several of these structures still stand, including the original Pioneer Station. (Courtesy Amador County Archives.)

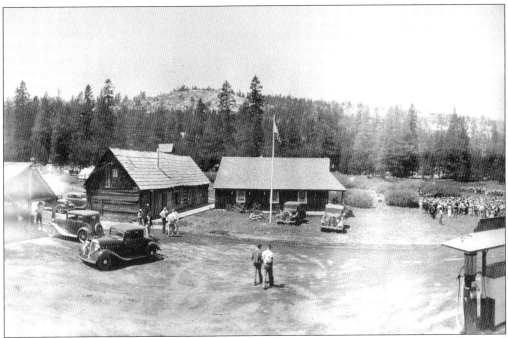

In this *c.* 1935 photograph at Plasse's Resort, a crowd gathers to celebrate Kit Carson Days and the 1844 John C. Fremont expedition. Carson Pass, of course, is named for Kit Carson. (Courtesy Amador County Archives.)

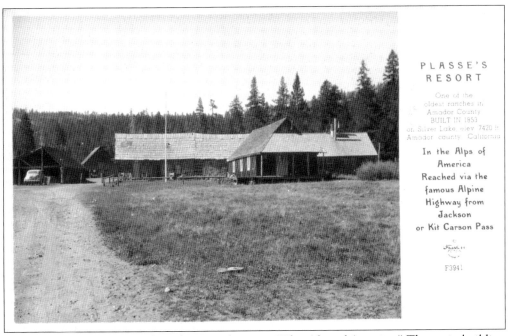

PLASSE'S
RESORT

One of the
oldest ranches in
Amador County
BUILT IN 1853
on Silver Lake, elev. 7420 ft.
Amador county California

In the Alps of
America
Reached via the
famous Alpine
Highway from
Jackson
or Kit Carson Pass

F3941

This *c.* 1940 postcard describes Plasse's as being in "The Alps of America." The main building pictured here, originally part of a ranch, was used as the resort's post office for many years. (Courtesy Amador County Archives.)

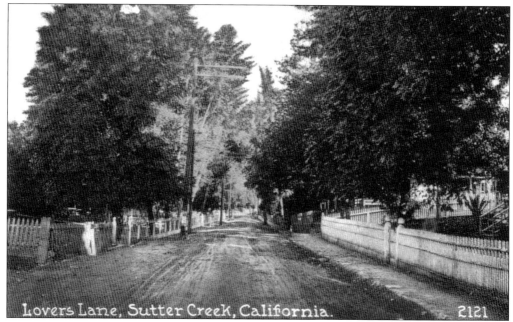

Lovers Lane, Sutter Creek, California. 2121

Sutter Creek is practically a booming metropolis these days, but as this *c.* 1920 postcard of Lovers Lane shows, it wasn't too long ago when the town was very rural. With all the open space around Sutter Creek, it is unknown why this particular Lovers Lane was in front of all these houses. (Courtesy Amador County Archives.)

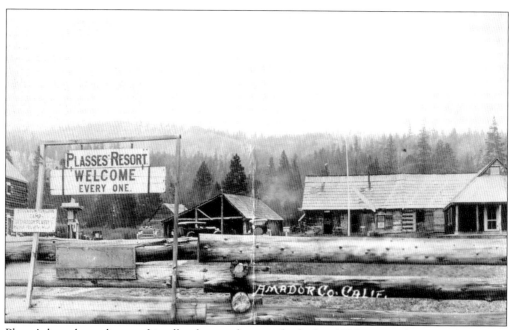

Plasse's has always been a friendly place, a fact to which this 1936 postcard attests. (Courtesy Amador County Archives.)

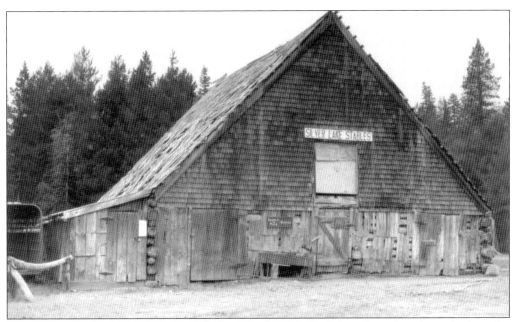

The area around Silver Lake is good for horseback riding and there have long been facilities for such around the lake. Pictured here is the Silver Lake Stables around 1970. (Courtesy Amador County Archives.)

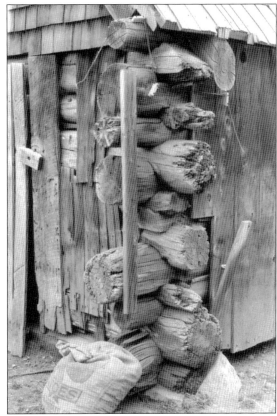

Here is the detail of a corner of the stables showing the building's log construction.

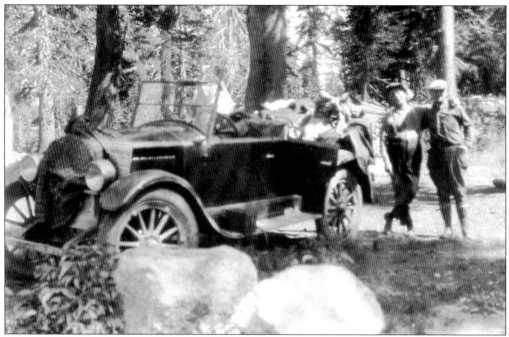

A couple of blades strike a jolly pose with a roadster near Silver Lake around 1923. The high elevations around Carson Pass were particularly challenging to cars in the early part of the century, with overheating common in the summer and traction problems in the winter. (Courtesy Amador County Archives.)

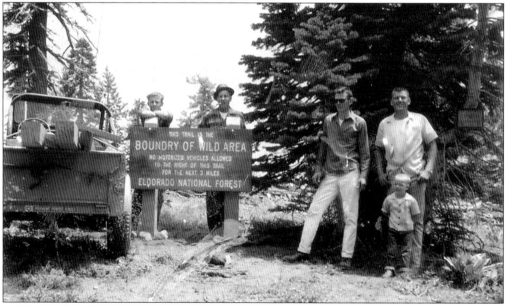

Some years later, the styles and the cars had changed but not the unstoppable upcountry spirit. Members of the California Association of 4-Wheel Drive Clubs stand next to a Jeep in the Eldorado National Forest around 1960. From left to right are Pete Hoose, Reed Sellers, Lee Chauret, Merle Moody, and an unidentified boy, trying to hide his disappointment that the Forest Service spelled "boundary" wrong. (Courtesy Amador County Archives.)

Time stands still, in a way, at Silver Lake, as very little development has gone on through the years. A few cabins are scattered around the body of water—most accessible only by snowmobile in the winter—but the shoreline is still pristine, looking very much today as it did when this image was taken in 1866. (Courtesy Amador County Archives.)

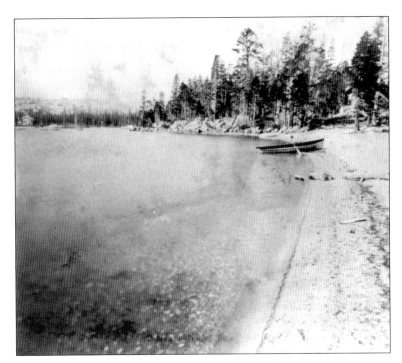

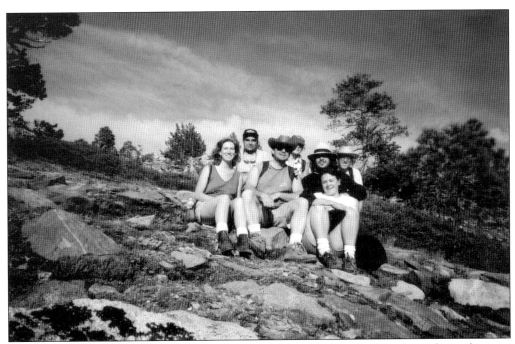

A group of hikers enjoys a summer afternoon in August 2002 on the Shealon Lake trail, across Highway 88 from Silver Lake. (Courtesy Miyuki Shinozuka.)

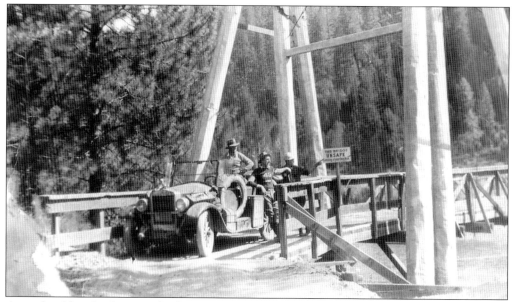

A gaggle of daredevils cross a bridge near Silver Lake in 1930, tauntingly pointing out a sign that reads, "This bridge unsafe—cross at your own risk." (Courtesy Amador County Archives.)

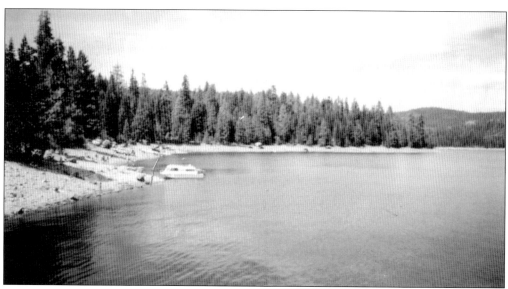

Bear River Reservoir is a man-made lake that is popular with boaters, campers, motorcyclists, and ATV riders. This 2004 image shows the lake's peaceful side, though it can be significantly more crowded. (Courtesy Lori Poultney.)

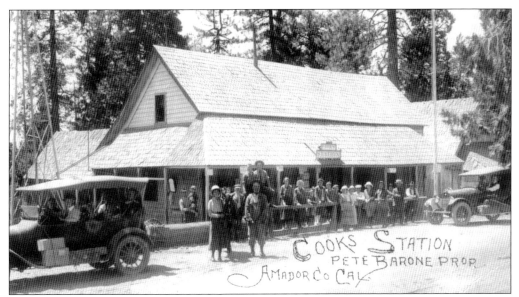

Cook's Station (at 5,000 feet) is a popular stopping place for gas and comestibles along Highway 88 to Silver Lake, Kirkwood, or Tahoe. This roadside stop got started around 1852 when Charlie Stedham built it to serve traffic heading down the Volcano cutoff of the Carson Emigrant Trail. The cutoff became a toll wagon road in 1863, and a number of way stations appeared along the route. Only Caples, Kirkwood, Cook's, and Ham's Stations (at 6,000 feet) remain of the 15 or so that were here in the 1860s. (Courtesy Amador County Archives.)

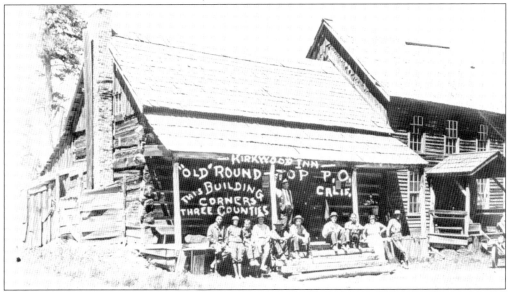

Also housing the Old Round Top Post Office (named for a nearby mountain), Kirkwood Inn is another of the original way stations along the emigrant trail. It was built in 1863 at the 7,800-foot level by Zack Kirkwood himself and still stands today. In 1864, Alpine County was created from segments of Amador, El Dorado, and Calaveras Counties, and the county lines converged in the dining room of the Kirkwood Inn. Legend has it that Kirkwood would confound tax collectors from the different counties arriving for their take of his liquor receipts by moving a bar on rollers into a different county within the same room. (Courtesy Amador County Archives.)

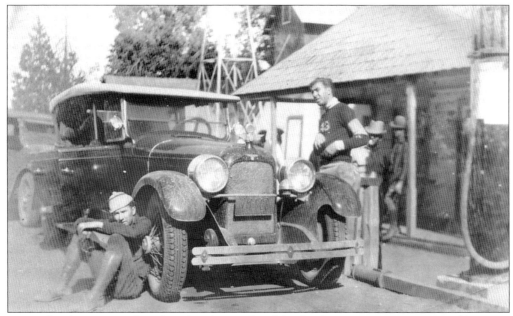

A couple of young toughs take a break outside of Cook's Station on June 8, 1930. (Courtesy Amador County Archives.)

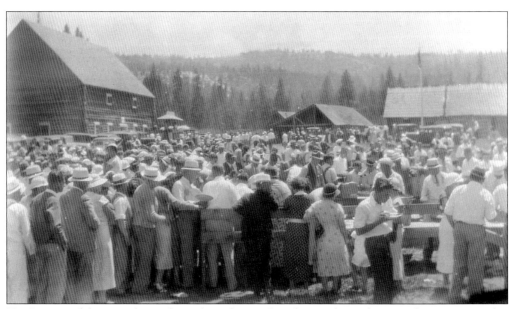

Kit Carson celebrations have always been big in Amador, as the earlier parade pictures in this volume illustrate. Here a large crowd gathers at Plasse's Resort in 1930 to commemorate the man himself, and on his home turf no less.

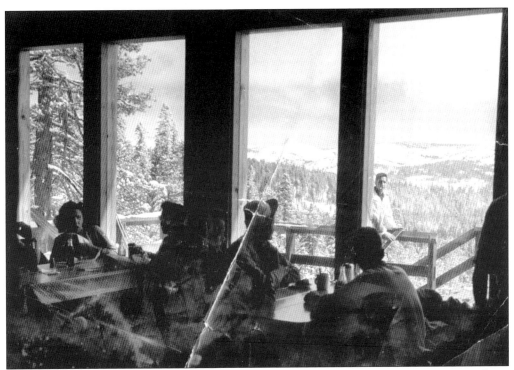

Peddler Hill Ski Lodge, pictured here c. 1955, was a ski area east of present-day Pioneer and was active from the 1940s until 1972 when Kirkwood Ski Resort opened 20 miles further up Highway 88 and usurped Peddler Hill's glory. (Courtesy Amador County Archives.)

Peddler Hill was the furthest that CalTrans would plow snow on Highway 88 until Kirkwood opened. Since then, the state maintains the highway all the way to Nevada, and Carson Pass is open year-round. As for the old Peddler Hill Ski Lodge, seen in this c. 1952 image, the site has been redeveloped as a CalTrans maintenance station. (Courtesy Amador County Archives.)

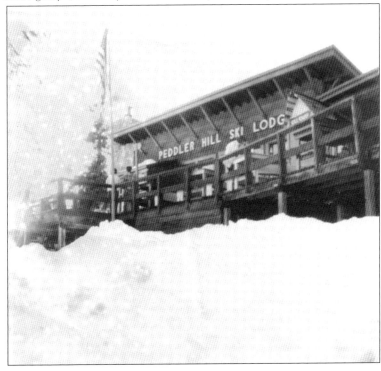

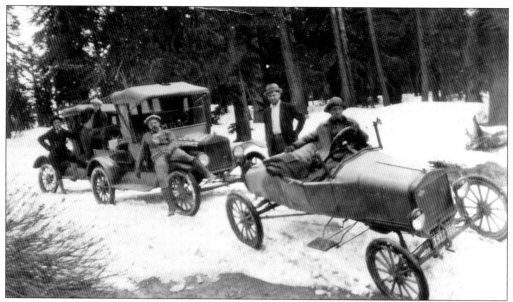

Snow is a fact of life in much of the upcountry, especially around Silver Lake where the elevation is 7,200 feet. In this June 1927 photograph, it is apparent that sometimes the snow stays around late in the year in the high country. (Courtesy Amador County Archives.)

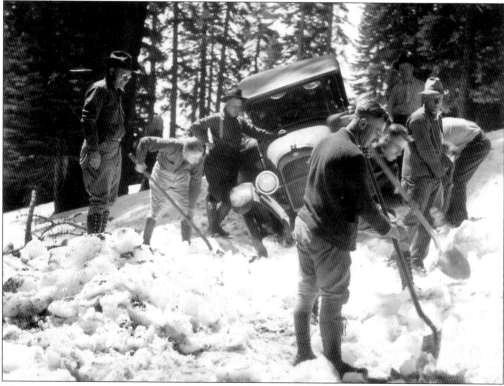

This group of 1927 motorists found out the hard way that snow sometimes makes travel difficult in the upcountry. This image was taken in June when it was thought the snow might have already melted. (Courtesy Amador County Archives.)

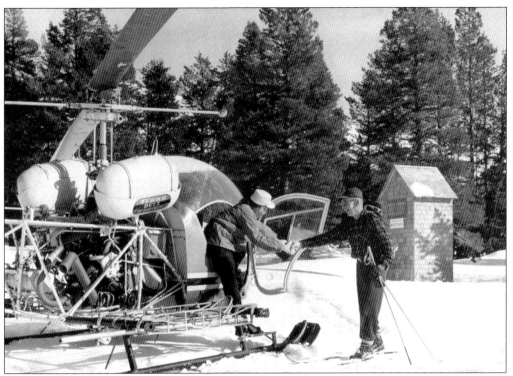

At times it's just plain easier—and friendlier—to go by helicopter, as this c. 1965 image near Silver Lake demonstrates. (Courtesy Amador County Archives.)

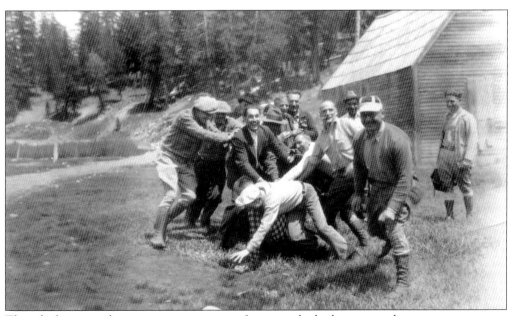

Though the winter brings copious amounts of snow to the high country, the summers are warm and mild. Here, in 1930, a boisterous group of men enjoys an unspecified sporting event at Plasse's. (Courtesy Amador County Archives.)

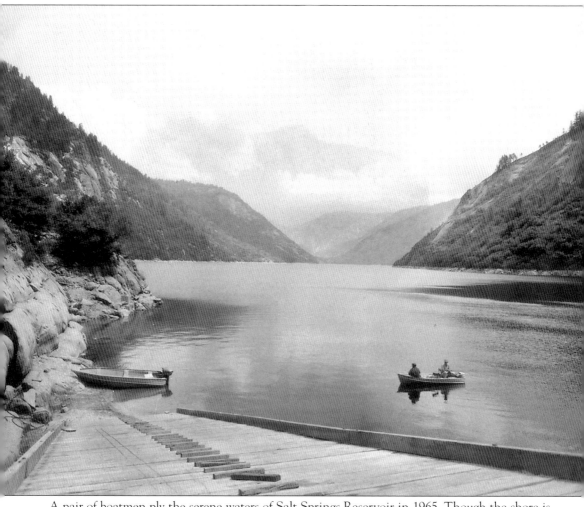

A pair of boatmen ply the serene waters of Salt Springs Reservoir in 1965. Though the shore is rocky around this lake, decent boating and fishing are available here. Strong afternoon winds make this an appealing spot for windsurfing as well. This lake is at 3,900 feet. (Courtesy PG&E.)

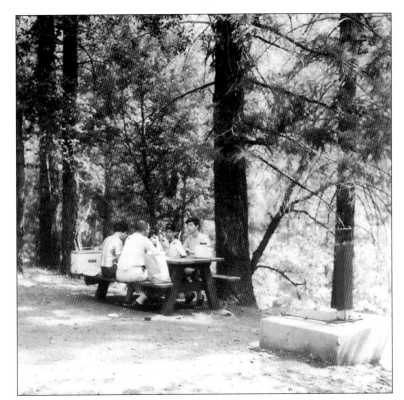

Amador's upcountry region, while never as popular as the neighboring Tahoe and Yosemite areas, nonetheless has a good array of camping and picnicking spots. A family relaxes at Tiger Creek in 1965 above, and a gathering of "mods" enjoys a campout at Silver Lake in 1970 below. (Courtesy PG&E.)

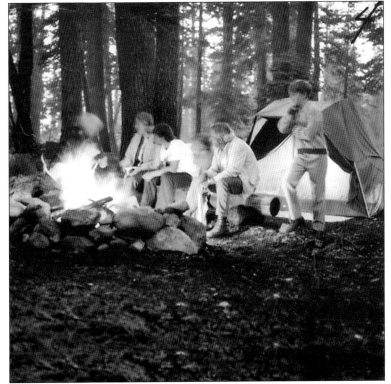

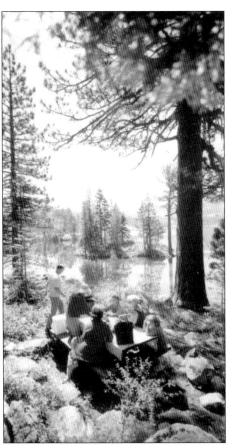

A family enjoys a picnic in 1965 at Silver Lake. Though the lake is largely undeveloped, a few amenities and accommodations (such as Plasse's and Kay's Resorts) are available. (Courtesy PG&E.)

The author performs preliminary research for this book on the Mokelumne River's north fork in August 2003, utilizing an early-model Budweiser raft with separately inflatable headrest. The 17-mile segment of this river between Salt Springs and Tiger Creek may soon be designated a National Wild and Scenic River as a part of Sen. Barbara Boxer's California Wild Heritage Act of 2006. Such a designation would protect it from future development. PG&E has already made some concessions to restore the river's natural flow levels while maintaining its hydroelectric power plants in the region. According to the U.S. Forest Service's Wild and Scenic Study of 1990, the Mokelumne's north fork contains many "extensive archaeological sites," and as the original trade route between various mountain tribes, presents in its unaltered form "a rare opportunity to study the cultural chronology, settlement, and linguistic history of the region." For more information on the north fork, or other natural aspects of the upcountry region, see the Foothill Conservancy's Web site at www.foothillconservancy.org. (Courtesy Lori Poultney.)

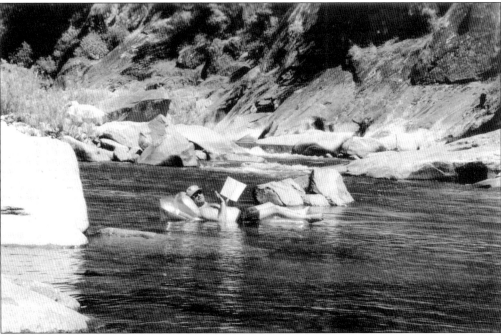

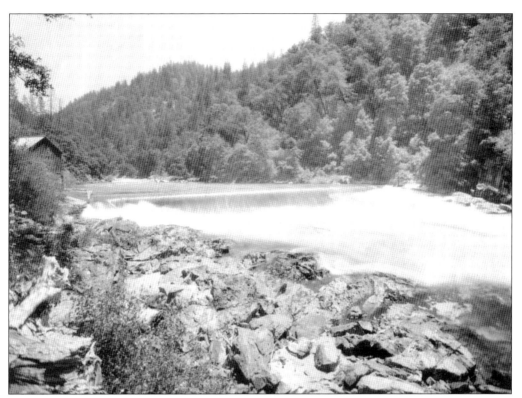

This diversion dam near the Tiger Creek powerhouse shelters a popular swimming and fishing area on the Mokelumne River. Kayakers going downstream from Salt Springs Reservoir must take out their boats and portage through this area because of the dam. This is the site as it appeared in 1931. (Courtesy PG&E.)

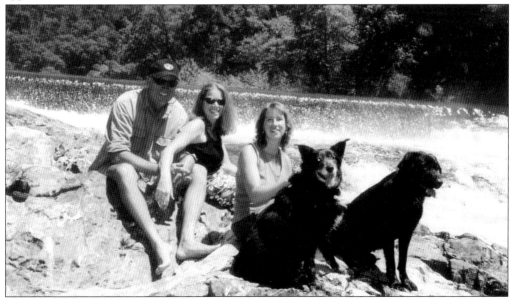

Seventy-three years later, a group of upcountry residents and their dogs enjoys a relaxing summer afternoon at Tiger Creek in 2004. (Courtesy author.)

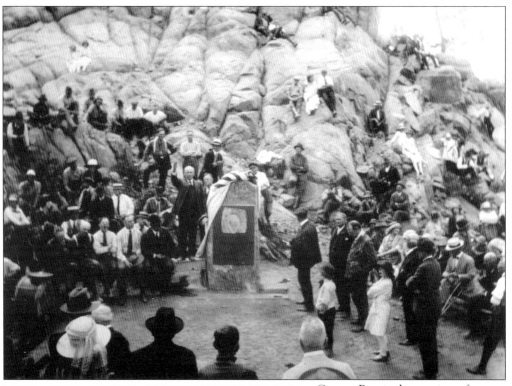

Carson Pass is the portion of Highway 88 that follows the trail established in the Sierras in 1879. This 1921 dedication ceremony commemorates one of the first state historic landmarks—the old emigrant trail. (Courtesy Amador County Archives.)

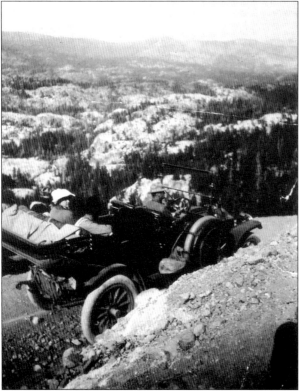

Travelers over Carson Pass in the early days had breathtaking views but also some challenging road conditions with which to contend. This c. 1928 image of a car heading over Carson Spur reads on the back, "Note the look of apprehension on the back seat driver's face." (Courtesy Amador County Archives.)

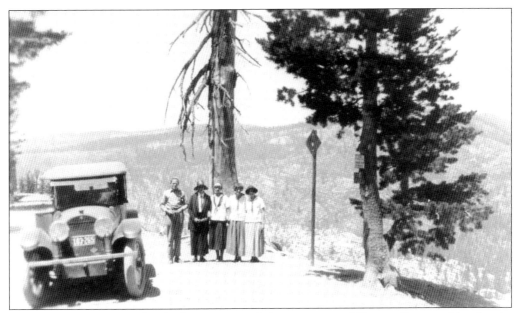

Sometimes one just needs a little scenery, and the area around Carson Pass provides that in abundance. Here a jaunty group enjoys the vistas from Carson Spur around 1925. (Courtesy Amador County Archives.)

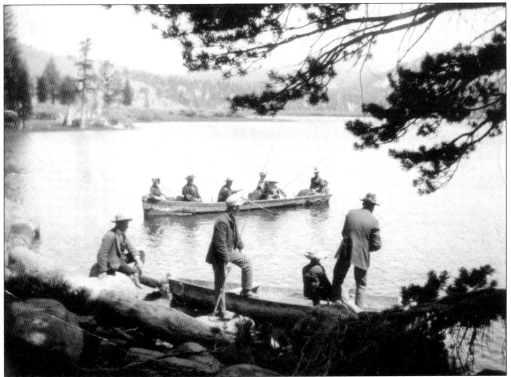

Warren Taylor (position in photograph undetermined), the grandson of Zach Kirkwood, fishes with a group of friends at Caples Lake near present-day Kirkwood around 1940. The poles are bamboo, which was standard equipment at the time. (Courtesy Amador County Archives.)

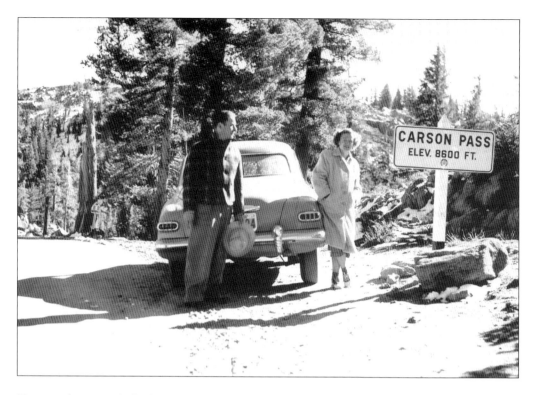

Two couples, one of which appears more advanced than the other, pose in the rarefied air atop Carson Pass, some 55 years apart. The above image was taken around 1950; the bottom is from 2005. (Above courtesy Amador County Archives; below courtesy author.)

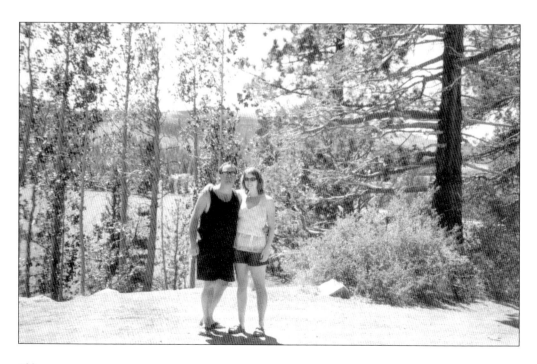

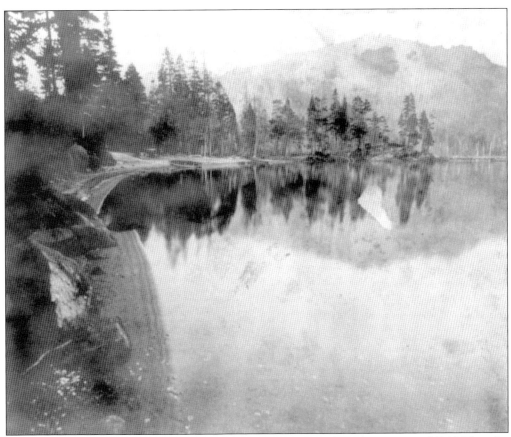

Serenity abounds at Silver Lake, as shown in this evening view from the summer of 1866. Thunder Mountain is in the background, reflecting on the lake. (Courtesy Amador County Archives.)

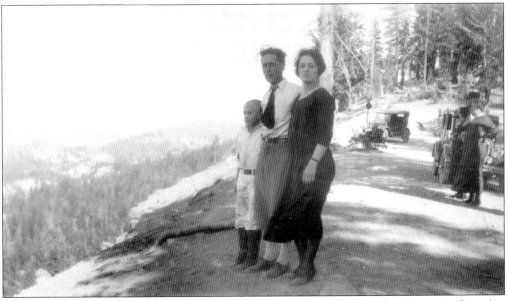

A family stops to enjoy the view from Carson Spur c. 1930. (Courtesy Amador County Archives.)

APPENDIX
STATE HISTORIC LANDMARKS
IN AMADOR COUNTY

MAIDEN'S GRAVE (State Landmark No. 28): This was said to be the resting placed of Rachel Melton, a young girl who in 1850 was accompanying her parents from Iowa to California via covered wagon when she took ill. In 2004, it was determined that a different member of the party was buried here and that Rachel is actually buried near Tragedy Springs. *Location: Highway 88, 10.5 miles west of Kirkwood, near mile marker 61.3.*

VOLCANO (State Landmark No. 29): The town grew up around a gold-mining spot called Soldier's Gulch, starting in 1848. By 1853, there were thousands here, along with quite a few hotels. Hydraulic mining did considerable damage to the land here. During the Civil War, a cannon named "Old Abe" was smuggled here via hearse to quell possible confederate sympathizers. *Location: Intersection of Main and Consolation Streets, Volcano.* (www.townofvolcano.com)

LANCHA PLANA (State Landmark No. 30): Lancha Plana (Spanish for "flat boat") was well settled by 1850, with extensive mining operations along the Mokelumne River's gravel beds. The *Amador Dispatch* newspaper, precursor to today's *Amador Ledger-Dispatch*, was started here in 1860. *Location: Camanche Reservoir north shore, about one mile west of County Line Bridge, six miles south of Buena Vista on Lancha Plana Buena Vista Road.*

DRYTOWN (State Landmark No. 31): The site of the first gold discovery in Amador, this town was founded in 1848, making it the oldest in the county. It was not actually a "dry" town—it had 26 saloons at one point. *Location: Highway 49, near mile marker 13.7.*

PIONEER HALL (State Landmark No. 34): The Native Daughters of the Golden West was organized at the site of the Pioneer Hall in 1886. *Location: 113 Main Street, Jackson.*

OLETA, also known as FIDDLETOWN (State Landmark No. 34): Founded in 1849, Fiddletown was a trading center for several mining camps. The settlement became Oleta in 1877, but the original name was brought back in 1932. The name is alternately credited to the "fiddling around" of young miners and to the musical variety of fiddling. An annual fiddler's jam is held here. *Location: South side of Main Street from Dr. Yee's Chinese Herb Shop, Fiddletown.* (www.fiddletown.org)

MIDDLE BAR (State Landmark No. 36): This was a gold rush town on the Mokelumne River, now normally flooded by the Pardee Reservoir at different times throughout the year. *Location: 2.8 miles south of Highway 49, on Middle Bar Road at Mokelumne River, 4.5 miles south of Jackson.*

CLINTON (State Landmark No. 37): This picturesque area was the center of a placer-mining community in the 1850s and of quartz mining through the 1880s. *Location: Intersection of East Clinton and Clinton Roads, 1 mile southeast of State Highway 88, 3.2 miles southwest of Pine Grove.*

IRISHTOWN (State Landmark No. 38): This region was a gathering point for miners heading to the southern gold fields. The early white settlers here found a "city of wigwams" and many mortars in the rocks. *Location: On Highway 88 near mile marker 20.8, 2.2 miles southwest of Pine Grove at Pine Grove Wieland Road.*

BUTTE STORE (State Landmark No. 39): These stone walls are the only remaining sign of the once-bustling mining town of Butte City. Proprietor Xavier Benoist had a store and bakery here as early as 1854, and Enrico Ginocchio had a store here later. *Location: Highway 49 near mile marker 1.4, 2.6 miles south of Jackson.*

KIRKWOOD INN (State Landmark No. 40): Originally built in 1863 by Zack Kirkwood, this landmark was a hotel, post office, and stage station. It was famed for having several county lines intersect in the barroom. *Location: Highway 88, near mile marker 71.8, Kirkwood.*

BIG BAR (State Landmark No. 41): This was a mining area along the Mokelumne River established in 1848. Starting in 1849, a ferry operated here until 1853 when the first bridge was built. *Location: Highway 49 at Amador/Calaveras County line, 4.0 miles south of Jackson.*

JACKSON GATE (State Landmark No. 118): This "gate" is named for a fissure in a rock that crosses the north fork of Jackson Creek. The first mining ditch in Amador was built at this spot in 1850 and approximately 500 miners worked here. *Location: North Main Street, 1.3 miles northeast of Jackson.*

SUTTER CREEK (State Landmark No. 322): Named for John A. Sutter, this town boomed in 1851 with the discovery of gold-bearing quartz. It was an important trading center for nearby mines and still is a very active town. *Location: Main and Badger Streets, at Veteran's Memorial Hall in Sutter Creek.* (http://ci.sutter-creek.ca.us)

PLYMOUTH TRADING POST (State Landmark No. 470): Joe Williams constructed this brick building in 1857. In 1873, the many small mines in the area were combined to become Plymouth Consolidated, and this was the new company's commissary and office. *Location: Main Street, Plymouth, between Mill and Mineral Streets, next to Wells Fargo.*

THE COMMUNITY METHODIST CHURCH OF IONE (State Landmark No. 506): This church was completed entirely from locally fired brick in 1866. It was first called the Ione City Centenary Church and later the Cathedral of the Mother Lode. It is listed on the National Register of Historic Places as NPS-77000287. *Location: 150 West Marlette Street, Ione.*

OLD EMIGRANT ROAD (State Landmark No. 662): At this high elevation (9,640 feet at one spot), the emigrant trail followed a loop around Silver Lake. It was a challenging stretch of road used by many thousands of wagons, walkers, and riders from 1848 to 1863. *Location: Highway 88, 8.7 miles west of Kirkwood, near mile marker 63.1.*

FIRST AMATEUR ASTRONOMICAL OBSERVATORY IN CALIFORNIA (State Landmark No. 715): George Madeira built an observatory near this spot in 1860 using a three-inch refractor telescope. He discovered the Great Comet of 1861 here and also reported on sunspot activity—the first reported astronomical research activity in the state. *Location: Volcano Town Hall.*

D'AGOSTINI WINERY (State Landmark No. 762): Swiss immigrant Adam Uhlinger started this winery around 1860. The present-day winery—one of over 30 in Amador—uses the original wine cellar with locally quarried rock wall, oak casks, and hand-hewn beams. A number of the winery's original vines are still in production, and the original building houses the Shenandoah Valley Museum. *Location: 7.2 miles northeast of Plymouth on Plymouth-Shenandoah Road.*

ARGONAUT AND KENNEDY MINES (State Landmark No. 762): These two mines, discovered in 1850 and 1856 respectively, were very important to California's early economic development, together producing over $105 million in gold. Kennedy's main shaft goes to 5,912 feet, and the Argonaut's goes to over 6,000 feet. The Argonaut was the site of the tragic Argonaut Mining Disaster in which 47 miners died at the 3,500-foot level as a result of a fire in the main shaft. *Location: Highway 49 roadside rest area, 1.6 miles north of Jackson, near mile marker 5.6.* (www.kennedygoldmine.com)

D. STEWART COMPANY STORE (State Landmark No. 788): Built in 1856 by Daniel Stewart, this general merchandise store was the first brick building erected in the Ione Valley area. Ione was a critical link on the main road to the southern and Mother Lode mines, despite its early, non-flattering names of Bed-Bug and Freeze-Out. *Location: 18 East Main Street, Ione.*

JACKSON'S PIONEER JEWISH SYNAGOGUE (State Landmark No. 865): The Congregation B'nai Israel of Jackson, dedicated at this site in 1857, was the Mother Lode's first synagogue. *Location: Southeast corner of Church and Main Streets, Jackson.*

PRESTON CASTLE (State Landmark No. 867): Opened in 1894, this imposing building is a splendid example of the Romanesque Revival style. It is alternatively known as the Preston School of Industry; this now-closed "castle" was actually a reform school by that name, created by the state legislature to house juvenile offenders. Like its early wards, the castle is currently being rehabilitated, but the School of Industry is still in use as a juvenile detention center. It is listed on the National Register of Historic Places as NPS-75000422. *Location: Currently closed to public, but a plaque is on Highway 104, 0.9 miles north of the castle, one mile north of Ione near mile marker 4.3.* (www.prestoncastle.com)

CHAW SE' ROUNDHOUSE (State Landmark No. 1001): This replica of a traditional Native American roundhouse, 60 feet in diameter, is one of the centerpieces of Indian Grinding Rock State Historic Park, which also features more than 1,100 mortar holes once used by native people to grind food and dyes. *Location: Chaw Se' Indian Grinding Rock State Historic Park, 14881 Pine Grove/Volcano Road, Pine Grove.* (www.parks.ca.gov/?page_id=553)

KNIGHT FOUNDRY (State Landmark No. 1007): A fascinating waterwheel–driven foundry and machine shop, Knight Foundry was created in 1872 to service and supply equipment to the mining and timber industries. Today it is restored and operable, showcasing the innovative use of high-speed waterwheels to operate industrial machinery. It is listed on the National Register of Historic Places as NPS-75000423. *Location: 81 Eureka Street, Sutter Creek.* (www.knightfoundry.org)

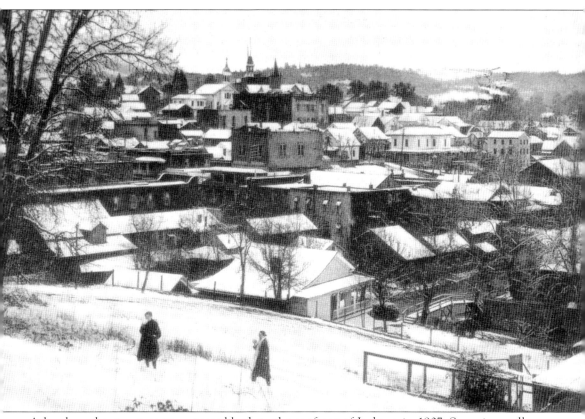

A lovely and not-so-rare snowstorm blankets the rooftops of Jackson in 1907. Snow is usually relegated to the higher elevations above Pine Grove, but it occasionally reaches the lower parts of Amador.

ACROSS AMERICA, PEOPLE ARE DISCOVERING SOMETHING WONDERFUL. THEIR HERITAGE.

Arcadia Publishing is the leading local history publisher in the United States. With more than 3,000 titles in print and hundreds of new titles released every year, Arcadia has extensive specialized experience chronicling the history of communities and celebrating America's hidden stories, bringing to life the people, places, and events from the past. To discover the history of other communities across the nation, please visit:

www.arcadiapublishing.com

Customized search tools allow you to find regional history books about the town where you grew up, the cities where your friends and family live, the town where your parents met, or even that retirement spot you've been dreaming about.

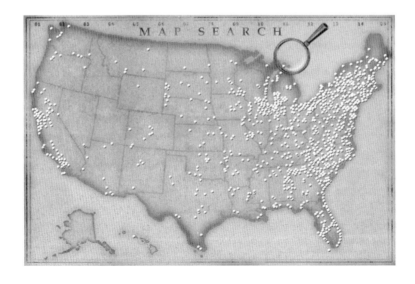